Thermopylae 480 BC

Last stand of the 300

Campaign • 188

Thermopylae 480 BC

Last stand of the 300

Nic Fields • Illustrated by Steve Noon

First published in 2007 by Osprey Publishing
Midland House, West Way, Botley, Oxford OX2 0PH, UK
44-02 23rd St, Suite 219, Long Island City, NY 11101, USA
Email: info@ospreypublishing.com

Osprey Publishing is part of the Osprey Group.

ISBN: 978 1 84176 180 0

Page layout by The Black Spot
Index by Alan Thatcher
Typeset in Helvetica Neue and ITC New Baskerville
Maps by the Map Studio Ltd.
3D bird's-eye views by The Black Spot
Battlescene illustrations by Steve Noon
Originated by PDQ Digital Media Solutions
Printed in China through World Print Ltd.

11 12 13 14 15   15 14 13 12 11 10 9 8 7 6

A CIP catalogue record for this book is available from the British Library.

The Woodland Trust
Osprey Publishing is supporting the Woodland Trust, the UK's leading
woodland conservation charity, by funding the dedication of trees.

www.ospreypublishing.com

Abbreviations

DNb	Dareios inscription from Naqš-e Rustam (b)
DPd	Dareios inscription from Persepolis (d)
DPe	Dareios inscription from Persepolis (e)
FGrHist	Jacoby, F. *Die Fragmente der griechischen Historiker* (Berlin & Leiden, 1923–58)
Fornara	Fornara, C.W. *Translated Documents of Greece and Rome I: Archaic Times to the end of the Peloponnesian War* (Cambridge, 1983)
GRBS	*Greek, Roman & Byzantine Studies*
IG	*Inscriptiones Graecae* (Berlin 1923–)
LACTOR	London Association of Classical Teachers – Original Records
NP	New Persian
OP	Old Persian

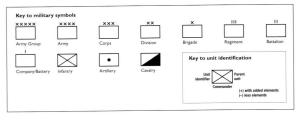

Key to military symbols: Army Group, Army, Corps, Division, Brigade, Regiment, Battalion, Company/Battery, Infantry, Artillery, Cavalry. Key to unit identification: Unit identifier, Parent unit, Commander, (+) with added elements, (-) less elements

Artist's note

Author's note

In the maps and bird's-eye view diagrams that accompany the
text, the Persian forces are shown in purple, and the Hellenic ones
in white.

Glossary

Antilabē	Handgrip of *aspis* (q.v.).
Aspis '	Argive shield', a soup bowl-shaped shield, some 80 to 100cm in diameter, held via an *antilabē* (q.v.) and a *porpax* (q.v.).
Corinthian helmet	Full-faced helmet formed out of a single sheet of bronze and lined with leather, the 'standard-issue' of its day.
Doru	'Dorian spear', a thrusting spear, 2 to 2.5m in length, armed with a spearhead (bronze or iron) and a *sauroter* (q.v.).
Epibatēs (pl. *epibatai*)	'Deck-soldier', hoplite (q.v.) serving as marine on a trireme (q.v.).
Helots	Indentured serfs who worked the land of Spartans and served as attendants and lightly armed troops in war.
Hoplite	Heavily armed foot soldier accustomed to fighting shoulder-to-shoulder in a phalanx.
Knemides	Greaves, bronze body armour for the lower legs.
Kopis	Single-edged, heavy, slashing-type sword shaped like a machete, the hoplite's secondary weapon.
Linothōrax	Stiff linen corselet, which is lighter and more flexible (but more expensive) than the *thōrax* (q.v.).
Mantis (pl. *manteis*)	Seer who accompanied the phalanx.
Othismos	Pushing stage of hoplite battle.
Panopliā	'Full armour', the panoply of a hoplite (q.v.).
Perioikoi	Free inhabitants who lived around Sparta but had no political rights, though liable for military service.
Polis (pl. *poleis*)	Conventionally translated as 'city-state', the term actually refers to an autonomous political community of Greeks.
Porpax	Armband of *aspis* (q.v.).
Pteruges	'Feathers', stiffened leather or linen fringing on corselet.
Sagaris	Scythian, single-handed battleaxe favoured by the Persians.
Sauroter	Bronze butt-spike.
Stratēgos (pl. *stratēgoi*)	General or commander of phalanx.
Thōrax	Bronze bell-shaped corselet, which is made up of front and back plates and flared at the waist and neck.
Trireme	Galley rowed at three levels with one man to each oar, the principal warship of the period.

CONTENTS

INTRODUCTION

To this day the three-day battle for the narrow defile of Thermopylae remains the stuff of legend, the heroic struggle where Leonidas, the Spartan king (and, as he believed, a descendant of lion-slaying Herakles himself), and 300 chosen men died bravely in their efforts to delay the Persians. Out of this do-or-die disaster sprung the belief amongst Greeks of a later generation that the Spartans obeyed their iron laws and never retreated, but this was a belief very largely created by the battle itself. It comes as no great surprise, therefore, to find that of all the battles in what the Greeks called the Median Events and we call the Persian Wars, pride of place is awarded to Thermopylae, one of those, to borrow the words of Michel de Montaigne, 'triumphant defeats that rival victories' (*On the Cannibals*, 1580). Dying on the battlefield was now seen as the ultimate Spartan virtue, and the image of the brave Spartans facing the Persian hordes at the rocky pass continues to inspire modern readers.

In antiquity the pass of Thermopylae, some 150km north of Athens and the last defensible corridor in Greece above the Isthmus of Corinth, was squeezed between the mountains on one side and the sea on the other. The heights there descend steeply into the pass leaving only a restricted route along the marshy coast. The pass itself narrowed in several places, and it was at the so-called Middle Gate, where previously the local Phokians had built a defence wall running down to the seashore, that the Greeks decided to make their stand with their bronze-faced shields and bristling hedge of spears. Archilochos' maxim that 'the fox knows many tricks, the hedgehog only one' (fr. 201 West) was mirrored by events, when a force of perhaps some 7,000 hoplites, with Leonidas as the commander-in-chief, held off the army of Xerxes for two days, until a local shepherd offered to guide the Persians to their rear by a mountain track, the Anopaia path. Informed of this by deserters and scouts during the second night, the Greeks divided, probably under orders, with some withdrawing; the surviving Spartans, Thespians and Thebans remained to act as a fighting rearguard.

When the Persians attacked on the third and final day, the Greeks first fought with their spears, and when their spears were shattered, they used their swords. When their swords were broken, they went after the Persians with bare hands and teeth. When Leonidas finally fell, the Greeks drove the enemy off four times before recovering his body. Indeed, before the Greeks made their last stand on a small mound, they killed many Persians 'of high distinction' (Herodotos 7.224.2) including two of Xerxes' half-brothers. The Thebans possibly surrendered at the last, but Persian arrows annihilated the rest. When he came upon Leonidas' body, Xerxes ordered the beheading of the corpse and the impalement of the severed head on a pole at the site of the battle. Thermopylae was the turning point of this part of the Greek and Persian wars; it raised the stakes of everything that would follow.

ORIGINS OF THE CAMPAIGN

The Persian empire was brought into existence suddenly by the victories of Kyros the Great (r. *c.* 550–530 BC) – almost as suddenly as it was to be destroyed little more than two centuries later by the victories of Alexander the Great. Like all empires it was founded on the ruins of others but, unlike those that had preceded it, instead of remaining confined within the territorial limits of the Near East the Persian empire expanded well beyond it. As vassals of the Medes, their kindred, the Persians had occupied the high valleys around Anshan, eastwards of what we still habitually call the Persian Gulf, which was then many kilometres inland of its present location.

East meets West in this Attic red figure kylix (Edinburgh, Royal Museum, 1887.213). Here a Persian foot soldier fights off a heavily armoured Greek hoplite. In the East the custom was to wear padded armour of linen or leather, which was lighter and more comfortable than that of the Greek 'brazen men'. (Esther Carré)

Persis (Fars), a land-locked country tucked beneath the Zagros range, the mountains that shelve from modern Iran to the Iraqi frontier, was poor and rugged. Naturally as hardy mountaineers, trained in the use of bow and sling, the Persians made excellent infantry, yet they required a leader able to transcend the petty chieftainships and harness their vigour and hardihood. Descending from his mountain kingdom, Kyros first overran the Medes to the north and then swiftly turned his attention westwards to the Lydian domains of Kroesos (546 BC). Having toppled the world's richest throne, the indefatigable Kyros returned eastwards to capture Babylon (539 BC), before meeting his death in an obscure war amid the Massagetai on the north-eastern frontier of his empire (530 BC). 'I am Kyros, who gave the Persians an empire, and was king of Asia', ran the cryptic epitaph on his modest stepped tomb. To the Persians of his day, it said enough.

His oldest son and successor, Kambyses, carried out his father's plans to conquer Egypt. Drawing from the seagoing people of his empire, the Asiatic Greeks and the Phoenicians, he organized a navy to sail on the Nile delta. Then mustering the veteran army forged by Kyros, he marched on Gaza and crossed the bleak desert strip beyond. A hard-fought battle at the Egyptian frontier post of Pelusium, in which Asiatic Greeks fought for both sides, decided the fate of the country (525 BC). Somewhere in Syria on his journey home, Kambyses passed out of history.

After a brief interlude of disorder and revolt, Dareios (r. 522–486 BC) conquered much of present-day Pakistan, embracing all the lands as far as the Indus, and then crossed the narrow waters of the Bosporos into Europe (513 BC). Although this foray was foiled by the trans-Danubian tribes, the army, which Dareios had left behind him on his return to Asia, conquered Thrace as far west as the Strymōn, and Macedonia, too, appears to have offered the Great King the symbolic 'earth and water', tokens of formal submission (512 BC). Despite the setback in the great flat spaces of Scythia, Dareios had obtained for Persia a valuable footing in Europe and pushed his boundaries to the very gates of mainland Greece.

A Persian and an Athenian fight over the body of a dead Persian, on a slab (London, British Museum, GR 1816.6-10.158) from the Athena Nike temple, Athens. Executed around 425 BC it has been suggested that the scene represents Marathon, a victory elevated to mythical status and ranked alongside such feats as defeating the Amazons. (Author's collection)

The Greeks first came into conflict with the 'arrow-bearing Medes' in Aegean Anatolia, as a result of the conquest of Lydia by Kyros. Following an abortive Lydian revolt in which some of them participated, many of their cities were taken by assault, and the rest were ordered to bend the knee to Persian rule, or else. It is recorded that the Spartans had sent an embassy to Kyros telling him rather grandly to keep his hands off their Asiatic Greek brethren. 'Who are the Spartans?' was Kyros' chilling response. The Asiatic Greeks decided to submit. Later, during the reign of Dareios, there was to be a widespread rebellion from Byzantion in the north to Cyprus in the south-east, the so-called Ionian Revolt (499–494 BC). Initially the Asiatic Greeks were surprisingly successful. This appears in part to have been due to the slowness of Persian mobilization. The rebels solicited aid from their kinsmen in mainland Greece, but only Athens and Eretria responded and they soon departed as the fortunes of war shifted to the Persians.

In the hinterland of Anatolia, with the advantage of interior lines of communication and superior numbers, the Persians were able to operate in more than one theatre of operations at once, and to use the river valleys as a means of attack; communications were much more difficult for the Greeks, who were isolated by the heights enfolding their sheltered littoral communities. The Persian high command also had the experience of conducting large-scale expeditions and thus the logistical know-how and the means to support their campaigning armies. Also, from Assyria the Persians had learned the finer skills of siege warfare, such as heaping mounds against city walls to overtop them. And so one by one the rebel states were reduced, often in a harsh manner, and, after five years, the revolt was extinguished. The Persians went on to complete the conquest of Thrace, including the Greek colonies that dotted its Aegean coast, and now, if not before, to bring even Macedonia under their control. All that remained to be done was to punish Athens and Eretria for their intervention or, as Dareios saw it, their brash impertinence.

If Dareios had Athens and Eretria as his immediate targets, his longer-range plans encompassed all Greece. Conquest of these states could be followed by the installation of puppet tyrants (ready at hand in

Schoenias, in the bay of Marathon, looking east towards Kynosoura. Returning from 20 years in exile, it was on this beach that Hippias stepped ashore with Datis believing he was going to be reinstated, with Persian help, as the tyrant of Athens. Herodotos tells us he lost one of his teeth in the sand. (Author's collection)

the case of Athens) true to Persian values and supported by Persian garrisons. Bridgehead established, it was then a matter of waiting for the next opportunity. So in 491 BC he sent envoys to Greece demanding 'earth and water' from everyone, including the Spartans, or beware the consequences. Resolved to take a tough line, the Spartans offered the Athenians an alliance and both of them executed Dareios' envoys, a serious breach of religious propriety as well as diplomatic etiquette. The Spartans are alleged to have flung his envoys down a well, telling them to get their earth and water for the king from there. Dareios next authorized a punitive strike across the central Aegean with a complete army on ship-board.

The following year a fleet of perhaps 600 ships, carrying possibly some 25,000 troops, including cavalry, first subdued the Cyclades, and then took Karystos and Eretria on Euboia. It was then a short dash across the strait to mainland Greece and Attica, where the expeditionary force made landfall at Marathon. With the Persian commanders as they stepped ashore, hungry for his long-lost position as tyrant of Athens, was the aging but now inspirited Hippias. Meanwhile the citizen army of Athens, rather than sitting tight, marched to engage the Persians at the point of invasion. After an eerie delay the Persians possibly began to move on Athens, and the Athenians with their Plataian allies, perhaps some 10,000 in all, were forced to fight. It was a triumph of David over Goliath. Yet Marathon was not the end of the war in Greece, merely the prologue to a series of bigger battles – Artemision, Salamis, and Plataia and, of course, Thermopylae.

Robert Graves was surely right to imagine that the Persian high command simply saw Marathon, which for the Athenians immediately assumed mythic status, as a minor setback in the grand scheme of things. Although the tone is light-hearted, his poem is actually a major work. Graves is a past master at capturing the exact tone of voice of the figure he wishes to lampoon. Here, the Persian speaker's words leave us in no doubt that the art of political 'spin' was alive and well several thousands of years ago. His pompous self-justification, though, betrays its own purpose:

Truth-loving Persians do not dwell upon
The trivial skirmish fought near Marathon.
As for the Greek theatrical tradition
Which represents that summer's expedition
Not as a mere reconnaissance in force
By three brigades of foot and one of horse
(Their left flank covered by some obsolete
Light craft detached from the main Persian fleet)
But as a grandiose, ill-starred attempt
To conquer Greece – they treat it with contempt;
And only incidentally refute
Major Greek claims, by stressing what repute
The Persian monarch and the Persian nation
Won by this salutary demonstration:
Despite a strong defence and adverse weather
All arms combined magnificently together.

Robert Graves, *The Persian Version*

The defeat of the Persian expeditionary force in 490 BC had by no means settled the issue. In cold fact Persian resources, immensely greater than those of any Greek state, remained unimpaired, and so Dareios now began planning the overland campaign, which would allow these resources to be brought to bear.

Dareios' death and the accession of Xerxes (486 BC) followed by a revolt in Egypt (485 BC), delayed matters, but by 481 BC massive preparations, shipbuilding and preparing of supplies and magazines, were in train. Likewise, a double bridge of boats was thrown across the Hellespont to avoid the time-consuming ferrying of Xerxes' army, another pontoon was placed across the Strymōn at Nine Ways in Thrace, and a canal was dug across the neck of land connecting the Mount Athos peninsula to Chalkidike to avoid the danger of the violent storms prevalent off Mount Athos: a Persian fleet had been wrecked off the promontory in 492 BC. Depots for storing supplies of food, fodder and military equipment were established along the Aegean coast of Thrace and in Macedonia. These preparations were quite open and if anything advertised to the Greek world that the Persian aim was clearly the subjugation of Greece, and if Greece submitted without a fight, so much the better. The future looked black indeed for Greece.

By the inexorable laws of empire, the Persian colossus had to expand or face contraction. Most men love power for its own sake, and for any man who has attained a position of absolute power, the desire to extend that power may be taken for granted. Power, as Henry Kissinger once observed, is for some an aphrodisiac. And so a decade after their reverse at Marathon, in 480 BC, the Persians were back, this time overland by way of Thrace and Macedonia, and led by the Great King in person. Thus, all things considered, the renowned oracle at Delphi, though often misleading and confusing, was perfectly justified in advising the Athenians to 'fly to the world's end' (Herodotos 7.140.2) rather than try to resist the Persian juggernaut.

CHRONOLOGY

559 BC	Kyros becomes king of Anshan.
556 BC	Birth of Simonides in Keos.
550 BC	Kyros conquers Media.
546 BC	Kyros conquers Lydia and Asiatic Greeks.
539 BC	Kyros takes Babylon after his victory at Opis.
530 BC	Kyros killed fighting Massagetai – accession of Kambyses.
527 BC	Death of Peisistratos – Hippias tyrant of Athens.
525 BC	Kambyses conquers Egypt.
	Birth of Aischylos in Athens.
524 BC	Kambyses attempts to conquer Kush.
522 BC	Polykrates of Samos overthrown by Persians.
	Death of Kambyses – Dareios seizes power in Persia.
518 BC	Birth of Pindar in Thebes.
513 BC	Dareios attempts to subdue Scythians.
512 BC	Dareios conquers Thrace.
510 BC	Hippias of Athens overthrown with Spartan help.
499 BC	Start of Ionian Revolt.
498 BC	Sardis (Lydia) burnt by Athenians and Eretrians.
497 BC	Persians crush revolt on Cyprus.
494 BC	Ionian fleet defeated at Lade.
	Destruction of Miletos by Persians – Ionian Revolt effectively ended.
	Spartans defeat Argives at Sepeia – Sparta supreme in Peloponnese.
493 BC	Persian victory at Malēne.
493/492 BC	Themistokles archon at Athens.
492 BC	Mardonios' operations in Thrace end in failure.
491 BC	Dareios demands all Greek states to submit to his rule.
490 BC	Persians sack Eretria (Euboia).
	Battle of Marathon.
486 BC	Xerxes becomes Great King.
486 BC	Revolt of Egypt.
485 BC	Revolt of Babylonia.
484 BC	Birth of Herodotos in Halikarnassos (Caria).
483 BC	Persians start to dig canal across neck of Mount Athos peninsula.
483/482 BC	Rich seam of silver found at Lavrion (Attica) – birth of Athenian navy.
480 BC	mid April: Xerxes leaves Sardis.
	late May: Greeks at Vale of Tempē.
	early June: Xerxes crosses Hellespont.
	late June: Xerxes holds review at Doriskos.
	late August: twin battles of Artemision and Thermopylae.
	early September: Xerxes enters Athens.
	late September: battle of Salamis.
	early October: Xerxes returns to Sousa.
479 BC	early June: Mardonios reoccupies Athens.
	mid July: Spartans mobilize.
	mid August: battles of Plataia (Mardonios is killed) and Mykale.
478 BC	Persians driven from Sestos and Byzantion (Chersonese).
476 BC	Persians driven from Eïon (Thrace).
472 BC	Aischylos wins first prize in Great Dionysia for *Persai*.
466 BC	Battle of the Eurymedon (Pamphylia).
465 BC	Assassination of Xerxes.
456 BC	Death of Aischylos in Gela (Sicily).
454 BC	Persians destroy Athenian expeditionary force in the Nile delta.
449 BC	Athenian Kallias arranges peace with Persia.
431 BC	Herodotos revisits Athens and dies not long afterwards.

OPPOSING COMMANDERS

To Xenophon, a keen hunting man, warfare constituted an expansion of the animal-hunting techniques common to pre-state warrior societies. And so the former Athenian mercenary-captain turned Peloponnesian gentleman-farmer set himself to enquire whether, in a more sophisticated world, the general (*stratēgos*) still ought to make his own person the example of his army's courage, or whether he ought not hold himself out of danger so that by observation and cool decision he could direct his army's efforts to best effect. After some discussion, he (*Oikonomikos* 21.4–9) comes to the conclusion that it is still best for the general to exhibit Homeric bravery, because of the example that gives.

There is an ancient Chinese proverb, which says: 'A general who is brave or stupid is a calamity.' In other words, soldiers ask more of a commander than mere bravery. Xenophon, conversely, having pinpointed the central dilemma of leadership, decides that deeds are far more important than thought. Keegan (1987: 315–338) lays down what he sees as the five basic categories of command: first, kinship, the creation of a bond between the commander and the commanded; second, prescription, the direct verbal contact between the commander and his men; third, sanctions, the system of rewards and punishments; fourth, the imperative of action, tactical/strategic preparation and intelligence; and fifth, the imperative of example, the physical presence of the commander in battle and the sharing of risk. The last category, the one we should keep foremost in mind when thinking of Thermopylae, can be sub-categorized into three command styles: commanders who *always*, *sometimes*, or *never* enter battle. At the two ends of the 'mask of command' spectrum we have the pre-state warrior chieftain of Homer exhibiting leadership in its most literal sense, and the battle manager who directs, as opposed to participates in, combat.

LEONIDAS, KING OF SPARTA

Leonidas (r. 489–480 BC), son of Anaxandridas, was probably born in the early 540s, to his father's first wife (name unknown) – but only after his father had had a legitimate son, Kleomenes, with a second – apparently bigamous – wife (again, name unknown). Herodotos wrote that Anaxandridas' bigamy was 'an unheard-of thing in Sparta' (5.37), but it certainly did not prevent Kleomenes assuming the throne on his father's death. After Kleomenes' birth Anaxandridas achieved, finally, successful conception with his original wife – procuring first Dorieus, and then two further sons, Leonidas and Kleombrotos. Thus Leonidas was one of four sons of Anaxandridas, the second born to his first wife, the third overall.

This modern statue of Leonidas was erected in 1968 at the expense of Greek Americans of Spartan origin. The statue is based on the 'Leonidas' found on the Spartan acropolis, which rises behind. Inscribed below is the two-word reply made to Xerxes when he invited the Greeks to lay down their arms. (Author's collection)

The fertile Eurotas valley, looking north-west from the Menaleion or Shrine of Menelaus and Helen. Sparta traces its origins in a group of villages on the banks of the river Eurotas in the southern Peloponnese. It grew by subjugating or enslaving its immediate neighbours in Lakonia and Messenia, who thus became helots. (Author's collection)

Leonidas, therefore, became king rather unexpectedly. He succeeded as the Agiad king of Sparta after the sinister death of his elder half-brother Kleomenes, whose heiress daughter, Gorgo, he had married. The official line was that Kleomenes took his own life in a fit of madness. Apparently he had sliced himself into pieces from the feet up, a sticky end brought about because he had become a demented alcoholic through having learned from some Scythian envoys to drink his wine neat. Wine for the Greeks was almost never taken neat; it was normally cut with water, the proportion of wine to water noted by ancient authors being 3:1, 5:3 and, at its strongest, 3:2. So by regularly taking his wine 'in the Scythian fashion', if that is what he did, Kleomenes was no better than the most barbarous of barbarians.

Yet the Spartans were notoriously abstemious and controlled wine drinkers, and the cult of Dionysos was certainly not ascribed to by them. The god of drunk, disorderly release was the very opposite of masculine Spartan control. Did Kleomenes jump – or was he pushed? It seems more likely that Kleomenes' reign was cut short by murder, arranged, and hushed up, on the orders of the man who succeeded him on the Agiad throne. It is possible that when Leonidas led out his small force to Thermopylae he had something on his conscience to expiate.

So it was while the rest of the Spartans were prevented by their over-riding obligation to celebrate their most important annual festival, the Karneia in honour of Apollo, that Leonidas marched north with a hand-picked body of 300 Spartans, all 'men who had sons living' (Herodotos 7.205.2). Of commands held by Leonidas previous to this one, which turned out to be his finest hour, we know nothing. As he was now beyond military age – the upper limit being 60 years – Leonidas could well have had experience of war stretching back to the 520s, but it could only have been in 'small wars', that is, against the Athenians and the Argives.

While Leonidas was preparing to make his stand, a Persian envoy arrived. The envoy explained to Leonidas the futility of trying to resist the advance of the Great King's army and demanded that the Greeks lay down their arms and submit to the might of Persia. Leonidas laconically told Xerxes, 'Come and get them' (*molōn labe*, Plutarch *Moralia* 225D). Though Leonidas repelled Persian assaults for two days, he failed to prevent his southern flank being turned via the Anopaia path. Dismissing the main body, he remained with 700 Thespians, 400 Thebans and the Three Hundred. The Spartans and the Thespians died to a man, and the Spartan king fell, pierced by Persian spears, while bravely leading a failed counter-attack.

Some 40 years later what were deemed to be his remains were brought back to Sparta for ceremonial reburial, and a hero-shrine was later established in his honour. As for the Three Hundred, their verse epitaph, composed by the most admired poet of the day, Simonides of Keos (b. *c.* 556 BC), and carved on a stone where they fell, is perhaps the most famous of all such inscriptions: 'Stranger, go tell the Lakedaimonians that here we lie, obedient to their laws' (Herodotos 7.228.2). This lapidary and suitably laconic couplet reminded all Greeks for generations to come of the debt owed to the Spartans. The same message of pride and defiance was conveyed by the stone lion marker erected at the site, since the king of the animal kingdom symbolized martial prowess. This monument was also an echo of Leonidas' own name, which means 'descendant of Leon'; *leōn* was the Greek for 'lion'.

A sixth-century pithos (Sparta, Museum of Archaeology) with a Spartan warrior. The Corinthian helmet, especially when burnished, presented a terrifying sight to the enemy. To add to the effect, Spartans would let their hair fall below their helmets. Once the universal custom, the wearing of long hair was now exclusive to Sparta. (Author's collection)

THE KINGS OF SPARTA

Sparta was an odd conglomerate of four village settlements (*obai*), with a fifth one being added at a later date, whose citizens liked to boast that they needed no walls. Yet the most peculiar fact about the Spartan state was its dual monarchy, a phenomenon that has never been satisfactorily explained. Herodotos (6.52.1) claims that the two royal families of Agiadai and Eurypontidai shared a common ancestor, both tracing their lineage back to the sons of the superhero Herakles, and thus were equally dignified. Another suggestion is that the two kings stemmed from a time when there were two tribes, each headed by a tribal chieftain. Eventually these tribes combined and the two chieftains shared the leadership. Herodotos (5.56–60) assures us that both kings shared equal powers, privileges and duties, and were the commanders-in-chief of the army for life. In other words, Sparta's dual kingship was a form of hereditary but non-monarchic military leadership, what Aristotle describes as 'a kind of generalship (*stratēgia*), irresponsible and perpetual' (*Politics* 1285a 4).

Likewise the Spartan political constitution was tribal in its make-up, with a warrior-assembly (*apella*) and a council of elders (*gerousia*). The latter consisted of the two kings and 28 members who were elected for life from those Spartiates who were 60 years of age and older. Little is known about the council's duties, though Herodotos (5.40) infers that it could serve as a court to hear capital cases. The *apella*, on the other hand, was made up of every Spartan warrior who had reached the age of 30. It sfunctions not only included electing members for the *gerousia*, but the election of another political body, which was made up of the ephors ('overseers'). The *apella* also had the ultimate sanction on matters of legislation and policy. The usual mode of voting was by acclamation, which even Aristotle considers a childish game show, though Thucydides (1.87.2) hints that this was not always the case.

The ephors, five in number, were freely elected each year and transacted much of the daily state business. They presided at meetings of the *apella*, received foreign ambassadors and transmitted orders to the commanders in the field. Their origin, however, is obscure. Xenophon (*Lakedaimonion politeia* 15.7) records that every month they and the kings exchanged oaths, each to uphold the position of the other, which suggests that in the distant, tribal past the ephors had functioned as shaman-type figures. Thucydides (1.131.2) says that the ephors had the power to imprison the kings, though not to judge and condemn, and Herodotos (5.39–40) demonstrates how far the ephors could indeed persuade the kings. Together, it suggests that the kings would bow to the combined will of the ephors and the *gerousia*. Perhaps when complaints arose against the kings, the ephors served as mere complainants and the elders as judges.

XERXES, GREAT KING OF PERSIA

The son of Dareios and Atossa, the daughter of Kyros, Xerxes (r. 486–465 BC) was designated by his father as heir apparent in preference to his elder half-brother Artabazanes – Xerxes was the first son born to Dareios after his accession to the throne (Herodotos 7.2.2). Xerxes is the Greek transliteration for the Old Persian *Xshayārshā*, the king's throne name, which is a compound of *xshayā*('king', cf. NP *shah*) and *ārshān* ('male', 'masculine') and so meaning 'king who is a true male', 'hero among kings'. Tall and handsome, the 32-year-old Xerxes certainly looked the part. And he followed in the footsteps of Kyros, his maternal grandfather and founder of the Achaemenid dynasty, so named for Achaemenes the semi-mythical founder of Kyros' clan. Every king since Kyros had led an invasion and every king had conquered new territory.

Xerxes is the Biblical king Ahasuerus, 'who ruled over one hundred and twenty-seven provinces stretching from India to Kush' (Esther 1:1), unquestionably the greatest empire in the history of the world to that date. Xerxes had also inherited from his father the plans for an expedition against Greece, and, as his accession was due not to primogeniture but selection, he faced the formidable task of confirming himself a worthy successor to Dareios. Having seized power after a bloody struggle against an individual said by him to have been the *magus* Gaumāta but who was, in all probability, Bardiya ('Smerdis' in Herodotos 3.61), full brother of Kambyses, Dareios, who came from a collateral branch of the Achaemenidae, went on to reorganize and consolidate the empire – as he records in the Bisitun Inscription – and established a beneficial despotism over its provinces.

Of course, few things could better earn the new king of kings respect than avenging his royal father against the Greeks. But this had to wait. At the beginning of his reign Xerxes had to deal with a revolt in Egypt (486 BC) and possibly one in Babylonia (485 BC). Though he fought successfully in Africa and Asia, Xerxes is customarily celebrated for his failure to conquer Greece, with the resultant loss of Macedonia, Thrace, and Aegean Anatolia (480–476 BC), and the crushing defeat at the River Eurymedon in southern Anatolia (466 BC). Yet he deserves a more sympathetic hearing. His expedition against the Greeks, to avenge Marathon but also reflecting an expansionist imperative, was elaborately prepared (roads were improved, a canal cut behind Mount Athos, the Hellespont bridged, and food dumps established) and of a large scale. Naturally, the Greeks were inclined to see in these elaborate preparations made by Xerxes no more than *hubris* – arrogance before the gods – which they associated with all despots and oriental monarchs. There is nothing to show that Xerxes and his high command were anything other than magnificent planners, on a scale undreamed of at that period of human history.

Herodotos' picture of a huge army incorporating every ethnically diverse part of the empire is quantitatively ludicrous, but no Near Eastern documents specific to the period survive that throw light on the recruiting, training, or equipping of Persian infantry or cavalry, and modern views diverge on how to replace it. There is little doubt that it was too large and cumbersome, and its logistical demands were surely ill suited to Greek topography. There is also a suspicion that too much reliance was placed on the expected brittleness of Greek unity. Although Xerxes was hardly the oriental hubristic despot that Greek writers depicted, there was enough arrogance in his nature to wish for a climatic battle to round off the campaign. It was not to be. The campaign floundered at 'divine Salamis' (Herodotos 7.141.4), where the Persian fleet fought on Greek terms, while Plataia again illustrated the advantage Greek hoplites had over Persian infantry when numerical superiority and cavalry mobility were neutralized by terrain.

Yet to the Persians, who saw the good rule of a king expressed in his building works, Xerxes was remembered as a great man. The more important buildings on the terraces of Persepolis, the spiritual and ceremonial capital, were completed in Xerxes' reign, including the audience chamber (Apadana) with its impressive limestone reliefs, illustrating the structure and extent of the empire: king, court, and endless thousands of subjects with their ethnographic characteristics. Xerxes' reputation as a weakling and a womanizer depends on certain recognizably novelistic passages in Herodotos (7.2–3, 9.108–113, who has little regard for Xerxes as a warrior who crushed rebellions in Egypt and Babylonia), and on the reading of royal inscriptions as personal messages by the Great Kings, rather than as formulaic royal statements. Seen from the heartland, his reign forms a period of consolidation, not of incipient decay or inbred decadence.

All the Greek writers were fascinated by the wealth and power of the Persian rulers, so they often recount, with much glee, stories of court intrigue and the moral decadence that comes from indulging in unlimited luxury. In such anecdotes, the Great King appears as an essentially weak figure, a prey to the machinations of powerful women and sinister eunuchs. This is an inversion of Greek social and political norms, with which we, as Westerners, have usually identified and still do so to this day – the binary oppositions of an 'us' and a 'them' so apparent during the recent conflicts in Afghanistan and Iraq. As such

A daric (London, British Museum) showing Xerxes wielding bow and spear. Armed and dangerous, this was the image of the Great King to be seen by millions who never saw him or his likeness otherwise. First introduced by Dareios, this coin of remarkably pure gold soon became the 'dollar' of its day. (Author's collection)

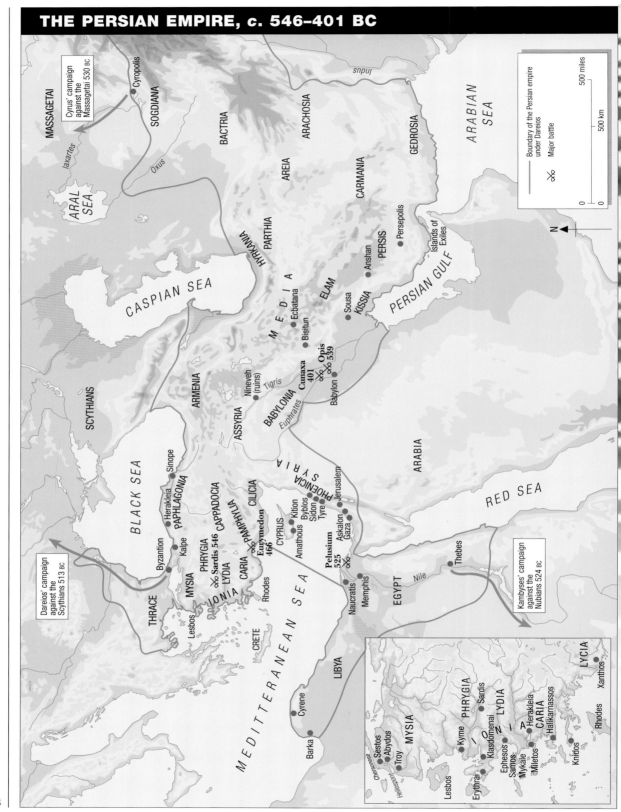

Indus

MASSAGETAI

Cyrus' campaign against the Massagetai 530 BC

Cyropolis

SOGDIANA

BACTRIA

ARACHOSIA

Iaxartes

Oxus

ARAL SEA

ARIA

HYRKANIA

PARTHIA

CARMANIA

GEDROSIA

ARABIAN SEA

Boundary of the Persian empire under Dareios

Major battle

500 miles

500 km

N

CASPIAN SEA

M E D I A

ELAM

PERSIS

Persepolis

Anshan

Islands of Exiles

PERSIAN GULF

Ecbatana

Bisitun

Sousa

KISSIA

Opis 539

Cunaxa 401

SCYTHIANS

ARMENIA

ASSYRIA

Nineveh (ruins)

Tigris

BABYLONIA

Euphrates

Babylon

ARABIA

RED SEA

BLACK SEA

Sinope

Herakleia

PAPHLAGONIA

Byzantion

Kalpe

CAPPADOCIA

CILICIA

S Y R I A

PHOENICIA

Jerusalem

Byblos

Sidon

Tyre

Kition

Amathous

CYPRUS

Askalon

Gaza

Pelusium 525

Sardis 546

Eurymedon 466

PHRYGIA

LYDIA

CARIA

PAMPHYLIA

MYSIA

IONIA

THRACE

Lesbos

Rhodes

CRETE

M E D I T E R R A N E A N   S E A

LIBYA

Cyrene

Barka

Naucratis

Memphis

EGYPT

Nile

Thebes

Dareios' campaign against the Scythians 513 BC

Kambyses' campaign against the Nubians 524 BC

Chersonese

Sestos

Abydos

Troy

Hellespont

MYSIA

Lesbos

Erythrai

Kyme

PHRYGIA

Klasdomenai

Ephesos

Samos

Mykale

Miletos

Sardis

LYDIA

Herakleia

CARIA

Halikarnassos

Knidos

Rhodes

LYCIA

Xanthos

I O N I A

the image of the cowardly, effeminate Persian monarch has exercised a strong influence through the centuries, making the Persian empire into a powerful 'other' in western orientalism, contrasted with 'western' bravery and masculinity. We must remember this in studying the Persian empire: the popular and widespread impression of its political system is fundamentally flawed.

The Great King was a warrior chosen, by other Persian warriors, from the Achaemenid clan, and in theory the succession passed from father to son. But a complicating factor was the multiplicity of sons always potentially available, thanks to the harem system developed by Xerxes. This was a vast organization overseen by the court eunuchs and contained both Persian and non-Persian wives. The Bible's Esther was one of these, and in the evening a young woman would go to Xerxes and 'in the morning return to another part of the harem to the care of Shaashgaz, the king's eunuch who was in charge of the concubines. She would not return to the king unless he was pleased with her and summoned her by name' (Esther 2:14).

Intrigue followed by assassination becomes endemic. Xerxes, together with his eldest son, would be murdered during a palace *coup d'état* in 465 BC (Ktesias *FGrHist* 688 F13, Aristotle *Politics* 1311b 37–40). Yet despite the defeat of his invasion, Persia was not excluded from playing an important role in Greek affairs. For the next century and a half most of the Asiatic Greek states remained firmly under Persian control, while Persian diplomacy and gold shaped the course of many political and military struggles in Greece.

The Bisitun Inscription

This exceptional document is a long text on Persian history, and is the only royal inscription that records facts, dates and places. It is engraved into a smooth rectangular section of cliff face of Mount Bisitun, some 66m off the ground, on the ancient caravan route and strategic highway between modern Hamadan (Iran) and Baghdad (Iraq). Bisitun, or Behistun, derives from the Old Persian word *Baga-stāna* and means 'the place where the gods dwell'. Mountains, as well as rivers, were regarded as sacred by the Persians, as well as the Elamites before them, and the inscription is certainly illegible from the ground. In those days, the road connected the capitals of Babylonia and Media, Babylon and Ecbatana (Hamadan).

The most famed of the Great Kings is Dareios, and like many famous men, he was not unduly modest. In this inscription Dareios commemorates his military victories. He tells us how the god Ahura Mazda (OP *Auramazdáhá*) chose him to dethrone a usurper named Gaumāta and save Persia, how he set out to quell several revolts, and how he defeated some foreign enemies. The monument consists of four parts. First, a large panel depicts a life-size Dareios, robed and armed with a bow, his bow-carrier Intaphrenes and his spear-bearer Gobryas, who can be identified as the father of Mardonios. Dareios overlooks nine representatives of conquered peoples, their necks tied by one long rope and their hands bound behind their backs. Another figure, badly damaged, is lying under Dareios' feet, and is labelled Gaumāta. Above these 13 people is a representation of the supreme god and principal deity of the Zoroastrian religion, Ahura Mazda. Underneath is a panel with a cuneiform text in Old Persian, a 'royal script' invented by Dareios in order to record his own native language, telling the story of the king's conquests. This text has a length of about 515 lines. There is another panel telling more or less the same story in Akkadian, the language once spoken in Babylonia and still used on official occasions and for scientific purposes. Yet another panel with the same text is written in Elamite, the language of the administration of the Achaemenid empire. This translation of the Persian text has a length of 650 lines.

After dethroning Gaumāta (522 BC), Dareios set out to quell several rebellions across the empire, which were quashed in 19 battles by a body of troops – the battle-hardened army that Kambyses had led to Egypt – loyal to him. The rebel rank and file were beaten down, and the captains, as usual, impaled after mutilation. This is also depicted above the text, where we see the god and the king, the slain usurper, and seven men representing seven rebellious people. While artists were making this monument, Dareios defeated several foreign enemies (520–519 BC); these victories were duly celebrated by a change in the initial design, adding two new figures, including the Scythian (Sakā) king Skunkha shown with long beard and pointed hat. When the carvings were completed, the ledge below the inscription was removed so that nobody could tamper with the inscriptions. Albeit a vital primary source for the history of Achaemenid Persia, the Bisitun Inscription is also a skilful piece of political propaganda, which served to legitimize the reign of Dareios.

OPPOSING ARMIES

When Aristagoras, the Persian-sponsored tyrant of Miletos, came knocking at the door of Kleomenes, king of Sparta, he had with him a map of the world, as he knew it, engraved on bronze. So armed, he then launched into an eloquent speech, which painted a vivid picture of the Great King's vast material wealth and the lack of valour displayed by his subjects. Of course the artful Aristagoras had good political reasons for doing so; he wanted Kleomenes to lend his support to a planned revolt of Asiatic Greeks from their overlord, Dareios. But Kleomenes refused to commit Spartan troops to a campaign against the Persian empire that might take them as much as three months' march inland from the familiar Aegean Sea, and ordered the Milesian out of Sparta before sundown. Aristagoras took himself off to Athens, where he had much better luck. Despite the boisterous tone of his two speeches, Aristagoras did touch upon two relevant facts about the Persian methods of warfare when he summed up their equipment as 'bows, short spears, trousers and turbans', and remarked that they had 'neither hoplite shield nor hoplite spear' (Herodotos 5.49.3, 97.1).

Yet the Persians were deemed invincible in the field by most people and, according to Herodotos, the Greeks had never yet stood their ground against a Persian army. During the Ionian revolt the Persians were to fight five land battles that we definitely know of and, interestingly, of those five they won four. Unfortunately the details are rather scarce in Herodotos. Of three (Ephesos, White Pillars, Labraunda) he offers no tactical information at all; one, in which the Persians 'were cut to pieces' (Herodotos 5.118), was a night ambush on a road near the town of Pedasos in Caria; and the final battle was the encounter at Malēne, near Atarnaios, on the mainland east of Lesbos. What little Herodotos says about this battle is intriguing, for while the Persian infantry were locked in combat the late arrival of the Persian cavalry tipped the balance and the 'Greeks fled' (6.29.1). Indeed, Herodotos later emphasizes the confidence of the Persians at Marathon in his remark that they thought the Athenians plain mad to risk an attack 'with no support from either cavalry or archers' (6.112.2).

When the art of classical warfare is reduced to its simplest elements, we find that there are only two methods by which the enemy could be defeated on the field of battle. Either the shock or the missile had to be employed against him. In the former, victory was secured through hand-to-hand struggle, and in the latter, via a constant and deadly rain of missiles that aimed to destroy or drive away the enemy before he could come to close quarters. And so battlefield weapons took on the characteristics that still define them: shock weapons like the stabbing spear, sword or axe, and projectile weapons such as stone, bow and arrow or throwing spear. Thermopylae would be a contest between two military systems, the close-quarter fighter (Greek hoplite) versus the long-range fighter (Persian bowmen).

THE GREEKS

The *polis* (pl. *poleis*), or the 'city-state', was the characteristic form of Greek urban life. Its main features were its small size, political autonomy, social homogeneity, and a real sense of community and respect for law. Yet the *polis* was not really a city, nor was it simply a town, as its population was distributed over a rural territory that might include many villages. It also emphasized people, the citizens, rather than territory. The distinctive sense of the *polis* was, therefore, a 'citizen-state' rather than a 'city-state'.

As the *polis* was always defined in terms of its members (e.g. the Athenians not Athens, the Spartans not Sparta), rather than geographically, it was, in essence, a community of warrior-farmers, males of military age who would necessarily fight for it, in which the military power of the community controlled the political and institutional life (magistracies, council, assembly). Because it was an agrarian-based society, the *polis* itself controlled and exploited a territory (*chora*), which was farmed by the citizens and their households. As the *chora* was delimited geographically by mountains or sea, or by proximity to another *polis*, parochial border wars were common. Autonomy was jealously guarded, but the necessities of collaboration made for a proliferation of foreign alliances, leagues, and hegemonies.

The citizen-militia

The armies of Greek *poleis* were based on a levy of those citizens (*politēs*) prosperous enough to equip themselves as hoplites, heavily armoured infantry who fought shoulder to shoulder in a large formation known as a phalanx – the word means 'stacks' or 'rows' of men. Except for the Spartans, who devoted their entire lives to military training, and a few state-sponsored units such as the famous, homoerotic Theban Sacred Band (comprising 300 men who were bound together by homosexual pairing), these citizen levies were untrained, part-time soldiers. It was the moral, social and, above all, political duty of a citizen of a *polis* to fight on behalf of his state in times of war. Liable for military service at any time from the age of 20, citizens remained on the state muster rolls for at least 40 years – desertion or cowardice could lead to loss of citizenship. Even a poet such as the Athenian Aischylos stood in the phalanx, and was, in fact, to be remembered on his grave as a warrior, not as a tragedian.

The hoplite panoply (*panopliā*) consisted of a large, round, soup-bowl-shaped shield (*aspis*), approximately one metre in diameter, a bronze helmet, a bronze or stiff linen corselet, and bronze greaves. The whole, when worn, could weigh in excess of 30kg, the heaviest individual item being the *aspis* at 7kg or thereabouts. Built on a wooden core, the *aspis* was faced with an extremely thin layer of stressed bronze and backed by a leather lining. The core was usually crafted from flexible wood such as poplar or willow. Because of its great weight the shield was

A Corinthian helmet (London, British Museum, GR 1873.9-10) of the very elegant 'final form' (c. 500 BC). This type was by far the most successful Greek helmet. Beaten out of a single sheet of bronze, it was close fitting, being shaped to the skull with only small openings for the eyes, nostrils and mouth. (Author's collection)

A mid sixth-century hoplite panoply (Olympia, Museum of Archaeology, B 5101, B 4985), consisting of a bronze bell-shaped corselet (left) and an *aspis* (right). This type of corselet took its name from the flange, which flared outwards below the waist like the mouth of a bell. The flanging helped to deflect incoming blows. (Author's collection)

carried by an arrangement of two handles: the armband (*porpax*) in the centre through which the forearm passed, and the handgrip (*antilabē*) at the rim. Held across the chest, it covered the hoplite from chin to knee. However, being clamped to the left arm it only offered protection to the hoplite's left-hand side.

Above the flat, broad rim of the shield, the hoplite's head was fully protected by a helmet, hammered from a single sheet of bronze, in the favoured Corinthian style. It had a long life, as it covered the face leaving only small openings for the eyes, nostrils and mouth, and yielded to a blow without cracking. A leather lining was fixed to the interior by the small holes pierced in the metal. Under the helmet many men wore a headband, which not only restrained the hair but also provided some support for this heavy piece of armour. Nevertheless, any hoplite wearing a padded bronze helmet in a hot climate was quite prepared to suffer considerable discomfort. Out of battle the helmet could be pushed to the back of the head, leaving the face uncovered. This is the position in which it most frequently appears in sculpture and vase paintings, and on coins.

A corselet, either of bronze or of linen, fully protected the hoplite's torso. The latter type of corselet was made up of many layers of linen glued together with resin to form a stiff shirt, about half a centimetre thick. Below the waist it was cut into strips (*pteruges*) for ease of movement, with a second layer of *pteruges* being fixed behind the first, thereby covering the gaps between them and forming a kind of kilt that protected the groin. First appearing in around 525 BC, the great advantage of the linen corselet (*linothōrax*) was its comfort, as it was more flexible and much cooler than bronze under the

The north frieze of the Siphnian Treasury, Delphi (c. 525 BC) showing the battle between the Giants, who are equipped as hoplites, and the Olympian Gods. Note the detail of the double-grip system of the *aspis*, an armband (*porpax*) fitted to the shield's centre, and a handgrip (*antilabē*) in the form of a strap near the rim. (Author's collection)

A bronze statue dedicated to the 700 Thespians who fell at Thermopylae. This force volunteered to stay with the Three Hundred, and probably comprised all the adult males of this small Boiotian *polis* who qualified for hoplite service. In a few short hours an entire generation of citizen-farmers was obliterated. (Author's collection)

Mediterranean sun. As far as protection goes, the main advantage of bronze was a surface that deflected glancing blows. A direct hit would punch through the metal, but it might be held up by any padding worn underneath. A linen corselet would not deflect glancing blows, but it would be as effective as bronze against any major thrust. This protection, then, was slightly less than that of bronze, but the advantages of comfort and weight overrode that consideration. Finally, a pair of bronze greaves (*knemides*) protected the lower legs of the hoplite. Shaped to imitate the muscles of the leg, these clipped neatly round the legs by their own elasticity. Thus the hoplite remained effectively armoured from head to foot.

The weapon *par excellence* of the hoplite was the long thrusting spear (*doru*). Fashioned out of ash wood and between 2 and 2.5m in length, the *doru* was equipped with a bronze or iron spearhead and bronze butt-spike. As well as acting as a counterweight to the spearhead, the butt-spike, affectionately known as the 'lizard killer' (*sauroter*), allowed the spear to be planted in the ground when a hoplite was ordered to ground arms (being bronze it did not rust), or to fight with if his spear snapped in the mêlée. The weapon was usually thrust overarm, the spear tip to the face of the foe, although it could be easily thrust underarm if the hoplite was charging into contact at the run. The centre of the shaft was bound in cord for a secure grip. The hoplite also carried a sword (*kopis*), a heavy, one-edged blade designed for slashing with an overhand stroke. Both the cutting edge and the back were convex, weighing the weapon towards the tip, but this was very much a secondary weapon.

Tactics

It was the hoplite shield that made the rigid phalanx formation viable. Half the shield protruded beyond the left-hand side of the hoplite. If the man on the left moved in close he was protected by the shield overlap, which thus guarded his uncovered side. Hence, hoplites stood shoulder to shoulder with their shields locked. Once this formation was broken, however, the advantage of the shield was lost; as Plutarch says (*Moralia* 241) the body armour of a hoplite may be for the individual's protection, but the hoplite's shield protected the whole phalanx. The phalanx itself was a deep formation, normally composed of hoplites arrayed eight to 12 shields deep. In this dense mass only the front two ranks could use their spears in the mêlée, the men in ranks three and back adding weight to the attack by pushing to their front. This was probably achieved by shoving the man in front with your shield. Both Thucydides (4.43.3, 96.2, cf. 6.70.2) and Xenophon (*Hellenika* 4.3.19, 6.4.14) commonly refer to the push and shove (*ōthismos*) of a hoplite mêlée.

In hoplite warfare, therefore, the phalanx itself was the tactic. When one *polis* engaged another, the crucial battle would usually be fought on flatland with mutually visible fronts that were not more than a kilometre or so long and often only a few hundred metres apart. Normally, after a final blood sacrifice (*sphagia*), the two opposing phalanxes would simply head straight for each other, break into a trot for the last few metres, collide with a crash and then, blinded by the dust and their own cumbersome helmets, stab and shove till one side cracked.

The skilful Spartans, according to the impressed Thucydides, were noted for their slow and ordered advance, marching in step the whole way to the rhythm of flute players and singing war songs, which contrasted with that of the enemy 'full of sound and fury' (5.70). Just before contact they would raise, in unison, a collective war cry (*paean*). The *paean* was a peculiarly Greek custom, Dorian in origin, but eventually adopted by the other Greeks. Aischylos describes it as a 'sacred cry uttered in a loud voice … a shout offered in sacrifice, emboldening to comrades, and dissolving fear of the foe' (*Seven Against Thebes* 268–270). The Spartans also wore crowns of foliage, at least up to the point where they halted to perform – much later than anyone else, and deliberately in sight of the enemy – their propitiatory blood sacrifice (Xenophon *Lakedaimonion politeia* 13.8, *Hellenika* 4.2.18, Plutarch *Lykourgos* 22.4). The slow march, war songs, shrill reed flutes and fresh garlands must have been an unnerving sight in the eyes of those looking from the wrong side of the battlefield. At this point it was not uncommon for the opposition to break and flee, that is, before actually coming 'within spear-thrust' (*eis doru*) of the Spartans.

Thucydides (5.71.1) also informs us that as the hoplite phalanx advanced it tended to edge to the right. The right-hand man would drift in fear of being caught on his unshielded side, and the rest of the phalanx would naturally follow suit, each hoplite trying to keep under the protection of his right-hand neighbour's shield. Thus each right wing might overlap and beat the opposing left. Thucydides implies that this was a tendency over which generals (*stratēgoi*), even in the Spartan army, had little or no control. At Thermopylae, as we shall see, this did not apply because the bare, right spear-side of Leonidas' phalanx was suitably guarded by the sea.

Hand-to-hand combat, close-quarter fighting, coming to grips or to blows, the Greeks delicately called all this the 'law of hands' (Herodotos 8.89.1). The mêlée itself was a toe-to-toe affair, the front two ranks of opposing phalanxes attempting to stab their spears into the exposed parts of the enemy, that is, the throat or groin, which lacked protection. Meanwhile, the ranks behind would push. As can be imagined, once a hoplite was down, injured or not, he was unlikely ever to get up again. This short but vicious mêlée was resolved once one side had practically collapsed. There was no pursuit by the victors, and those of the vanquished who were able fled the battlefield. It was enough, as the philosophers noted, every so often to kill a small portion of the enemy in an afternoon crash, crack his morale, and send him scurrying in defeat and shame whence he came.

Ritual

Hoplite battles had a strong ritual character; the idea was to defeat rather than to annihilate. So, forget strategy and tactics. Fighting a set-piece battle on the flattest piece of terrain, hoplites would physically push the enemy from the pitch, a point clearly made by Mardonios (OP *Marduniya*), son of Gobryas and Dareios' sister, in a speech to his cousin Xerxes:

> [T]he Greeks are pugnacious enough, and start fights on the spur of the moment without sense or judgement to justify them. When they declare war on each other, they go off together to the smoothest and flattest piece of ground they can find, and have their battle on it.

Herodotos 7.9, ß.1

On pottery, especially Attic red figure, skirmishers are normally shown wearing the everyday dress of Greek shepherds, namely a tunic of coarse, woollen cloth and a shaggy felt hat. Wearing no armour, their sole means of defence was a makeshift shield formed by an animal pelt laid across the left arm and secured into place by knotting a pair of the paws around the neck. Lacking the specialist training to use bow or sling, their weapons seem to be restricted to stones or javelins; only occasionally do we find the odd representation of a figure carrying a sword, which was perhaps plundered from the battlefield.

A Greek javelin was often provided with a leather thong (*ankyle*) midway along the shaft. The thong would be fixed onto the shaft with a temporary hitch knot and formed a loop that was hooked round the first two fingers of the skirmisher; the other two and the thumb gripped the shaft. When the weapon was cast, the loop unwound and was, consequently, retained in the hand. The throwing-thong imparted extra speed to the javelin as well as rotation for stability in flight. In Greek iconography, the typical javelin thrower's hold with the first two digits straight outstretched together is very distinctive.

Although Mardonios believed that the Greeks pursued their unique style of warfare out of ignorance and stupidity, what he says is incontrovertible. As it turned out, he would lose both his life and his army.

But why did the hoplite style of head-to-head, open-terrain fighting last so long? For a start, the fighting was taking place on the hoplites' own land. In addition, as time passed the system was maintained for the sake of tradition, shared values and social prejudice. Hoplite warfare was for prestige rather than for the survival of a *polis*. Sparta, whose warriors were acknowledged as the past masters of this style of warfare, was an exception to the rule – its hoplites were permanent and essential rather than occasional and ritual. Indeed, there were implicit rules of engagement, the 'common customs', for Greeks fighting Greeks. These rules included the following: war was to be declared before hostilities; hostilities were sometimes deemed inappropriate (e.g. during religious festivals); some places were protected, as were some persons (e.g. shrines, heralds); trophies were to be respected; the dead were to be returned; non-combatants were not a legitimate target; fighting was to take place in

A manikin (Paris, musée de l'armée, #2) of a Greek hoplite. The hoplite shield (*aspis*) covered the bearer from shoulder to knee, and more than anything else made the phalanx possible. Note the distinctive convex shape of the *aspis* with its flat, offset rim, which provided rigidity to the bowl of the shield. (Esther Carré)

The east frieze of the Siphnian Treasury, Delphi (*c.* 525 BC), which shows the Trojan heroes Aineias and Memnon, who are both depicted as hoplites. The details of the equipment are authentic, and Aineias (the left-hand figure) wears a stiff linen corselet, while Memnon (the right-hand figure) retains the older, and heavier, bronze bell-shaped corselet. (Author's collection)

The north frieze of the Siphnian Treasury, Delphi (*c.* 525 BC). These Giants, equipped as hoplites, employ the overarm thrust with the *doru*. The shaft was made of ash, and the spearhead (bronze or iron) was balanced by a bronze spike at its butt end. The weight of a 2.5m *doru* was about 1kg. (Author's collection)

proper season; and there was to be only a limited pursuit of defeated and retreating foes. These rules did not apply to 'barbarians', non-Greek speakers, and they would break down during the Peloponnesian War (Krentz 2002).

The Greeks developed what has been called by Hanson the 'Western Way of War' – a head-to-head collision of soldiers on an open plain in a magnificent display of courage, physical prowess, honour, and fair play, and a concomitant repugnance for decoy, ambush, sneak attacks, and the involvement of non-combatants. There was also no honour for the Greeks in fighting from afar. An archer or a javelin thrower who launched his weapon from a great distance was not held in high esteem, because he could kill with little risk to himself. Only those who clashed with spear and shield, defying death and disdaining retreat, were deemed honourable.

Attic red figure kylix (Athens, Agora Museum, P 42) attributed to the Chaerias Painter and dated *c.* 510–500 BC. This scene decorating the fragmentary tondo of the cup depicts a young hoplite pouring a libation before an altar. No Greek army marched without a strong sense of the gods as onlookers and guides. (Author's collection)

The hoplites went into battle not for fear of punishment or in hopes of plunder and booty. The hoplites were the citizens of *poleis* who owned property – usually farms – and held certain political rights. They fought to defend their liberties and home and hearth. They fought side by side with neighbours, brothers, fathers, sons, uncles and cousins. This meant that they did their utmost to demonstrate courage side by side with their comrades and that they had a vested interest in the outcome – they stood to lose everything. Hoplite battle was brutal and personal. Armed and armoured hoplites advanced in their phalanxes and fought to the death. Their battle-fields were scenes of furious fighting and carnage that usually consumed not more than an hour or two. Every man was pushed to the limits of his physical and psychological endurance – and then it was over, not to be repeated for a year or more.

The Spartan Agōgē

At birth it was the elders of the tribe (*gerontes*) who decided on grounds of health if a newborn Spartan child should be reared – the grim alternative being exposure on the mountainside. The boys who passed inspection were deliberately toughened from an early age, by bathing them in wine, feeding them with plain fare and getting them accustomed to harsh conditions. Then from the age of seven (Plutarch) or 14 (Xenophon) there began a state-organized upbringing, the *agōgē* ('raising'), aimed at preparing them for their future role as warriors. The boys were organized into 'packs' (*agelai*) under pack leaders, which in turn were supervised closely by magistrates. The boys were brutally initiated into communal living, providing, for example, their bedding from reeds cut by hand from the banks of the shallow, sandy Eurotas. They were also prohibited everyday luxuries such as footwear, allowed only one cloak to wear throughout the year, and survived on a diet that

A fifth-century limestone relief (Chalkis, Museum of Archaeology, 7) from Larymna, Evvía (Euboia), depicting a pre-battle sacrifice of a ram. The single stroke of the sacrificer's sword, normally a *mantis*, anticipates the bloodshed of the battle and marks its ritual beginning – the killing of the animal is immediately followed by the killing of men. (Author's collection)

A sixth-century bronze *porpax* (Olympia, Museum of Archaeology). The left arm was put through this band, thus securing the *aspis* to the forearm of the hoplite. The *antilabē* near the rim, grasped with the left hand, helped him manage the great weight of his shield and stopped it slipping down the forearm. (Author's collection)

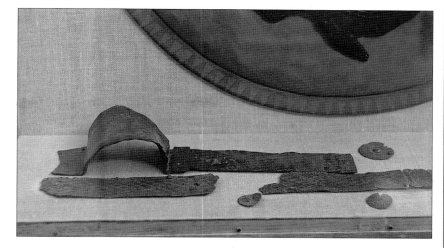

Fifth-century, leaf-shaped spearheads (London, British Museum, GR 1865.7.53-54) of bronze. The narrower end of the *doru* shaft was fitted with the spearhead, pitch being the primary means of securing it in place. Some spearheads, like the bottom example here, also have round nail-holes as a further means of attachment. (Author's collection)

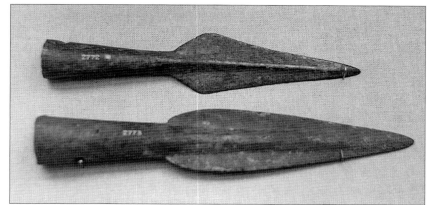

Bronze butt-spikes (Delphi, Museum of Archaeology, 10854, 10871-72), two ending as cylindrical tubes, and one as a rectangular talon. The butt-spike not only enabled the *doru* to be planted upright in the ground when not in use, but also could be used offensively in the event of the spearhead snapping off. (Author's collection)

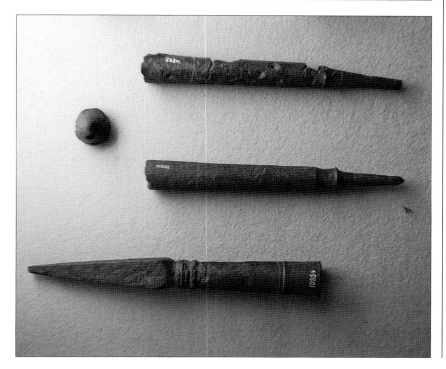

was deliberately inadequate. The latter hardship promoted the stealing of food as an adventurous duty, which in turn led to severe beatings if a boy was caught in the act. Formal education was kept to a minimum, but did include music, gymnastics, and games embracing the principles of warfare (Xenophon *Lakedaimonion politeia* 2–4).

Spartiatai

These were the Spartan warriors, who, at the age of 20 and having survived the *agōgē*, were elected into one of the military messes, variously called *sussitia*, *andreiā* or *phidition*, also known as common tents or *suskania*. But it was only at the age of 30 that he was admitted to the full rights of a citizen as one of the 'equals' or 'peers' (*homoioi*) and allotted an estate, or lot (*klēros*), on which his household would be supported by the labours of helots ('captives'). Though the Spartiates were in theory considered equals, in practice there were differences in birth and wealth. Aristotle (*Politics* 1270b 6–7) says that only certain families were eligible for membership of the *gerousia*. Likewise, land ownership was not on an equal basis either despite Plutarch's claim (*Lykourgos* 8.2) that Lykourgos divided the land into equal lots (*klēroi*). Although we must be wary of Plutarch's more lurid details, life for the Spartiate was certainly vigorous. Thucydides, who is not noted for his extravagance, has Perikles compare the 'laborious training' (2.39.1) of the Spartan with the easier life to be had by an Athenian. It is clear the Greeks themselves were well aware of the main reason for the superiority of Spartan hoplites. For instance, Herodotos describes them as 'past masters' (7.211.3) in warfare, what Thucydides calls their 'practised skill' or 'experience' (4.33.2). Unlike most Athenians, who thought the Spartans a pretty dreadful lot, Xenophon, who spoke as an eyewitness, admired them as 'the only true craftsmen in matters of war' (*Lakedaimonion politeia* 13.5).

An early sixth-century terracotta metope (Sparta, Museum of Archaeology) depicting Spartan hoplites. A fully armoured Spartiate slowly advancing to contact spoke of reassuring discipline and obedience. But the blood-coloured tunic and oiled tresses, a terrifyingly beautiful sight in its own right, also evoked a more primitive world of hunting and death. (Author's collection)

A detail from the left-hand frieze of the Thermopylae monument. The story of Thermopylae is the *locus classicus* for the iron discipline and die-hard bravery of the Spartans, and the complete indifference with which they went about daily chores despite the dangers ahead. Their death, moreover, created the myth of the doomed army that prefers death to surrender. (Author's collection)

Such is Xenophon's diagnosis of the key point in Spartan military professionalism, but he was the enemy of luxury, the admirer of bravery and military prowess and the champion of moral life, including the common bond of hunting. It is left to that arch-rationalist Aristotle to actually put his finger on the heart of the matter. He explains (*Politics* 1338b 27–30) that it is not so much the methods the Spartans used to train their young men that made them superior, as the fact that they trained them at all. That this was also true of the adults is the crux of a witty anecdote told by Plutarch (*Agesilaos* 26.4, *Moralia* 214A), and repeated by Polyainos (2.17). On one occasion, having received bitter complaints from Sparta's Peloponnesian allies about the comparative scarcity of the troops that it had fielded, Agesilaos ordered the whole army to sit down. The Spartan king then asked first the potters, then the smiths, then the carpenters, then the builders, and so on, to stand up, until almost all the allied hoplites were on their feet, but still not a single Spartiate. The point, of course, was that the contingent of the allies was composed of essentially part-time soldiers, the Spartan of full-time professionals that knew no other trade. Sparta was an odd community isolated from surrounding fashions, yet life was not quite as grim as Plutarch paints it, and the Spartans were certainly not all blood and iron. Pindar, the Theban lyric poet, wrote of Sparta that the 'dances, music, and exuberant joy flourished alongside councils of old men and the spears of young men' (fr. 199 Snell).

Male bonding

In the ancient Greek world, the specialized and continuous military training was the preserve of Sparta and, in some cases, of those states that kept small bodies of elite troops. It must be emphasized, however, the skill-at-arms of the individual Spartiate was not the most important part of his training; rather, this was his being part of a coherent unit. The simplicity of hoplite warfare left little scope for the display of personal skills. When, for example, Xerxes quizzes Demaratos about the martial nature of his fellow Spartans, the latter admits that the Spartans fighting as individuals are as good as the next man, but fighting together are the 'best of all men' (Herodotos 7.104.4). Thus, at Thermopylae, only troops trained to move as one and instantaneously execute the words of command could have carried out those series of feigned retreats described by Herodotos (7.211.3).

The bedrock of military *esprit de corps*, comradeship in the Spartan army was extremely strong. According to Spartan tradition, the reforms of Lykourgos, the omni-provident lawgiver who brought about 'good order' (*eunomia*) in Sparta (Herodotos 1.65), had been most particular in fostering it. The *agōgē* initially fostered comradeship and belonging as one of its cornerstones. Young boys were drilled in packs. Having survived the *agōgē*, a young Spartiate sought membership to one of the military messes. This *syssition*, as it was sometimes called, comprised some 15 members who spent considerable time with one another, even when not in training. It was here, of course, that they dined communally and ate simple food including the notorious black broth (Plutarch *Lykourgos* 12.7).

Xenophon's fictitious Kyros the Great, undoubtedly thinking of the Spartans, considered that those who messed together would be less likely to desert each other, and that there could be no stronger phalanx than one composed of comrades (*Kyropaideia* 2.1.28, 7. 1.30). Athenaios, albeit using second-hand evidence unlike Xenophon, even says the Spartans made preliminary sacrifice to Eros in front of the battle lines 'with the belief that safety and victory lies in the love of those ranged alongside each other' (13.561e). Whether or not we are prepared to accept the real possibility that sometimes the feelings of Spartans for their comrades were homosexual, though the Greeks themselves did not have a notion of a 'homosexual nature', the fact remains that the basic male bonding process is built upon mutual self-respect and a special kind of love that has nothing to do with sex (i.e. Kipling's 'passing the love of women') or even idealism. Besides, unlike the Theban Sacred Band, homosexual couples were not customarily stationed next to each other in the phalanx.

When on campaign, the *syssition* was the Spartiate's 'cloak and camp-bed', and was undoubtedly the basic building block for the formation of the *enomotia*, the smallest unit in the Spartan army with a nominal strength of 40 men. Compare the Athenian army, for instance, where the *taxis*, the tribal contingent of some 1,000 men, was divided only into a number of sub-tribal units, the *lochoi*, each of which almost always contained at least several hundred men. In other words, an individual Spartiate ate, slept and fought side by side with comrades he had probably known since his boyhood days, and it was these comrades good opinion that counted more strongly with him than the mortal fear of the enemy. 'Small group cohesion' is a complex chemistry of individual and collective needs, loyalties and pressures that can urge men to go forwards or stand firm even in the face of certain death. Personal honour is one thing valued more than life by the majority of tribal warriors. The same also could be said of the Thespians at Thermopylae.

This finely worked, life-sized marble torso of a hoplite (Sparta, Museum of Archaeology, 440) wears a Corinthian helmet with cheek pieces shaped like rams' heads. It has been considered by many scholars to have formed part of the memorial that was erected on the acropolis of Sparta to honour Leonidas on his reburial. (Author's collection)

THE PERSIANS

The Persians (OP *Pársá*) whom Kyros united, tough mountaineers from an impoverished region, did not possess a professional army. As in days of old, the 'people' of a region were represented by its backbone, the 'military force', so the two words were used synonymously in one Old Persian term, *kárá*, a sense still retained in the New Persian term *kas-o kar* ('relatives and supporters'). At first the Achaemenid army consisted wholly of warriors of Iranian stock, and even when other regions were subjugated, Iranians formed the nucleus of the imperial army. Dareios, the third Great King, advised his successor:

> *If you should think: 'May I not fear anybody', protect the Persian* kárá.
> *If the Persian* kárá *are protected, continuous happiness for a very long time will come down towards this house.*

DPe 3

Dareios was a self-made man who took power in a *coup d'état*: a builder not a destroyer, he went on to become a mighty conqueror, a brilliant administrator, a religious visionary, an architectural genius, and creator of the world's first large-scale coinage. On surveying his world, Dareios, a determined and perennially cool personality, could boast:

> *This country, Persia, which Ahura Mazda bestowed upon me, is good, and possesses good horses and possesses good soldiers. By the favour of Ahura Mazda, and of me, Dareios the king, it does not feel fear of any other.*

DPd 2

It was, of course, a selective view, but the king of kings could afford to be selective. Absolute master, sole fountain of authority to his people, his word was law across dominions so vast they diminished Greece to territorial insignificance. With the expansion of the petty kingdom of Persis into an empire embracing all Iranian groups from central Asia to the Danube, a standing army was formed from Persians, Medes, and closely related peoples, and an imperial or grand army was organized by incorporating warriors of all subject nations.

Representations found in the Apadana at Persepolis, and official Persian economic and military documents were ultimately used by Herodotos to prove that the closer a nation was to the Persians, the more it shared in the domination of the empire by paying less tribute but contributing more soldiers. Thus, the warlike Medes, who had once exasperated the Assyrians and now held the second position in the empire, furnished more soldiers than others. Indeed, many of the imperial generals were chosen from the Medes (Mazares, Harpagos, Taxmaspada, and Datis). Next up were the Scythians (OP *Sakā*, Gr. *Sákai*), Iranian-speaking nomads who were phenomenal bowmen and scalped their enemies, and then the Bactrians, Hyrkanians and other eastern Iranian groups.

Old Persian inscriptions regularly distinguish two Scythian subject peoples, the *Sakā Tigraxauda* ('Scythians wearing pointed hats') and *Sakā Haumavarga* ('Scythians who brew/drink/venerate haoma').

This section of the Alexander Sarcophagus (Istanbul, Arkeoloji Müzesi, 370 T), Royal Necropolis Sidon, shows a Persian soldier wearing the *tiara*, a soft cloth hood with two lappets tied under the chin and a third at the neck. Commoners wore the peak flopping to one side; to wear one's *tiara* erect was equivalent to laying claim to the throne. (Author's collection)

Herodotos mentions Scythians with 'tall pointed hats set upright on their heads' (7.64.2) as coming to Greece with Xerxes, and these warlike people are usually located in the vicinity of the Caspian and Black Sea. Earlier in his *Histories* Herodotos had described in a full and picturesque manner their customs and way of life, and their dress came to be standard uniform for eastern archers and Amazons in Greek art. A third group, the *Sakā Paradraya* ('Scythians beyond the sea'), were those encountered by Dareios in the course of his Scythian campaign beyond the Danube and thus remained unconquered.

The standing army

The general term for the standing army was *spada*. This consisted of infantry (OP *pasti*), cavalry (OP *asabari*, horse-borne) and occasionally camels (OP *usabari*, camel-borne), and charioteers (though only the noblest warriors used the then obsolete but symbolic chariot), all of which was accompanied by a large number of camp followers. From the moment they met the Greeks (OP *Yaunā*, Ionians, cf. *Javan* mentioned in Genesis 10:1), the Persians incorporated subject or mercenary Greeks in their army. As the time went by, not only Persian satraps in Anatolia and the Levant but also the Great King himself employed Greek mercenaries as bodyguards (Gr. *doruphóroi*, spear-bearers) each of whom, theoretically, received free board and a monthly wage – according to Xenophon (*Anabasis* 1.3.21) a gold daric per month in 401 BC. By the time of Alexander the Great, these mercenaries were to become a regular part of the *spada* and their leaders, men like Memnon the Rhodian, were incorporated into the Persian aristocracy. They played a major role in Graeco-Persian cultural relations, and helped an eastward expansion of Hellenic culture.

The organization of the *spada* was based on a decimal system far superior to anything on the Greek side and was not employed in any Asiatic army until the Mongols and the 'fearsome hordes' led by Genghis Khan. Ten men composed the basic tactical sub-unit, a *dathabam*, unit of ten, under a *dathapatiš*, commander of ten; ten of these units made up a *satabam*, unit of one hundred, under a *satapatiš*, commander of one hundred; ten of these units formed a *hazarabam*, unit of one thousand, under a *hazarapatiš*, commander of one thousand; and ten of these units comprised a *baivarabam*, unit of ten thousand under a *baivarapatiš*, commander of ten thousand. But some caution is needed here. The last term is purely speculative and survives only in Avestan, a language closely related to Old Persian. We do hear of the Persian 'myriad' (Gr. *murias*), which stood for 'countless numbers' in the Greek sources much as we use loosely millions or billions. In summary:

Number of troops	Name of unit	Title of commander
10,000	*Baivarabam*	*Baivarapatiš*
1000	*Hazarabam*	*Hazarapatiš*
100	*Satabam*	*Satapatiš*
10	*Dathabam*	*Dathapatiš*

The spada was led by a supreme commander. This was probably the *spadapatiš*, although a generalissimo with full civil authority was often called *karana* (Gr. *karanos*), who was either the Great King himself or a trusted near- or blood-relative. A characteristic of the Achaemenid period is that commanders and dignitaries participated in actual fighting, and many of them lost their lives in action, as did Kyros in Scythia and Mardonios at Plataia. Lower commands also were a family affair. Eleven sons of Dareios, for instance, took part in the invasion of Greece, and three were killed during it: Abrokomas and Hyperanthes, junior officers, who both fell at Thermopylae, and Ariabignes, admiral of the Ionian and Carian naval contingents, who went down with his ship at Salamis.

Serve to lead

The training of the Persian nobility was arduous. After spending the first five years of their lives away from their fathers in the company of their mothers and other women of the household, they were then taught to be soldiers and leaders. The young Persian was schooled in running,

The Alexander Sarcophagus (Istanbul, Arkeoloji Müzesi, 370 T), Royal Necropolis Sidon. The mainstay of Persian armies was the foot soldier equipped with a short spear, composite bow and lightweight wicker shield. A Persian army could deliver a stupendous missile barrage, so the desire was to let the men shoot for as long as possible. (Esther Carré)

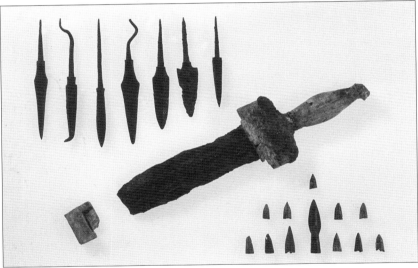

Arrowheads, spearheads, and an *akinakes* (London, British Museum, 108723, 108772-774, 108766) from Deve Hüyük, Syria. The *akinakes* was a long, double-bladed dagger, hung, according to Herodotos (7.61.1), from a waist belt and secured to the right thigh with a thong. Also hanging from the waist, but on the left, was the *gorytos*. (Author's collection)

swimming, horse grooming, tilling the land, tending the cattle, performing various handicrafts, and getting accustomed to standing at watch. He would be trained in the arts of the chase, both on foot and on horseback, archery, throwing the spear and javelin, and of sustaining forced marches under adverse conditions. Here we should note Herodotos' famous observation that the scions of Persian nobility 'are carefully instructed from their fifth to their twentieth year, in three things alone – to ride, to draw the bow, and to speak the truth' (1.136). Xenophon (*Kyropaideia* 1.2.10) echoes these Persian educational ideals when he observes that the pursuit of hunting also prepared the young nobleman for the hardships of soldiering: it gave him courage to face the dangers of the battlefield; it practised him in the use of the tools of their trade, that is, the spear and the bow; it acquainted him with the rigours of marching and running; and it meant he could endure the elements.

Around the age of 20 the Persian youth embarked upon his military career, which lasted until he was 50, either as a foot soldier or as a horseman. The elite, from the top down, were trained for both tasks. Dareios, therefore, is proud to say of his youthful education:

> *I am trained in my hands and in my feet; as a horseman, I am a good horseman; as a bowman, I am a good bowman, both on foot and on horseback; as a spearman, I am a good spearman, both on foot and on horseback.*

DNb 9

The physical abilities of the Great King are thus stressed – he is a supremely able rider, and can wield the bow and spear both on foot and on horseback with consummate skill. Dareios wished to be regarded as the first man in the realm, rightly so, and thus the first to contribute those abilities that were valued highest in Persian society, as they ensured the defence and preservation of the empire. Fighting and hunting was a way of life, and we find the same martial qualities ascribed by Xenophon (*Anabasis* 1.9.5) to Kyros the Younger, the rebel prince he once served.

The Persian infantry

The mainstay of fifth-century Persian armies was the foot soldier. He carried a long, straight, double-edged dagger, the *akinakes* of Herodotos (3.118.2, 128.4, 7.61.1, 9.107.2) and Xenophon (*Anabasis* 1.2.27, 8.29); a short spear with wooden shaft and metal head and butt, the latter a spherical counterweight; and a quiver full of arrows of reed with bronze or iron heads, and a composite bow. The latter was housed in what the Greeks called a *gorytos*, a smart combination of bow case and quiver holder that had been invented by the Scythians. Worn at waist level, the *gorytos* had two separate compartments: one held the bow and the other was a pocket for arrows that could be tightly closed with a flap.

Persians also employed a battleaxe (Gr. *sagaris*) 'like those which the Amazons carry' (Xenophon *Anabasis* 4.4.16), the Amazons being a race of female warriors who disdained to cohabitate with the male sex. Again of Scythian origin, the *sagaris* had a long, slender handle with a heavy cutting or striking blade or point. It took a number of different styles but it was characteristically a lightweight weapon that could be used by both horsemen and foot soldiers. It was a useful sidearm to carry, being light enough to be used effectively one-handed but still able to penetrate a metal helmet or body armour.

The composite bow, the Persian weapon *par excellence*, was quite large by contemporary standards (perhaps 1.2m long). Xenophon (*Anabasis* 3.3.7, 15, 4.17) himself was witness to the fact that Persian archers could easily outrange the Cretans, the most famous specialist archers of antiquity, but noted that later the Cretans practised long-range shooting at a high trajectory with captured Persian arrows. This suggests that the greater Persian range was the result of lighter arrows and different training, rather than any difference in bow technology. Cretan archers used large, heavy arrowheads with barbs, whereas Persian heads were usually three-edged, some three to four centimetres long, and socketed. The socketed heads were fitted to a wooden fore shaft, which was in turn

inserted into the main shaft, which was light, hollow, and made from
reed. With their small heads, these relatively lightweight arrows were
more effective against unarmoured targets than penetrating shield or
body armour.

Even so, as a symbol of kingship and the Persian national arm, the
bow was held in the hand of the Great King in his sculptures and on his
coins. Hence he could boast, 'I will conquer Greece with my archers.'
This was something of a pun, intentional or otherwise, as the gold daric
coin (Gr. *dareikós*) was popularly known by the Greeks as the 'archer'.
The obverse of this golden coin bore the device of a crowned 'running
archer', a man dressed in the Persian calf-length tunic, holding his bow
and arrow ready to shoot with one knee bent as if in motion – the Great
King himself, armed and ready.

The 'drawn bow' stands in Aischylos' *Persai* (147–148) as a symbol for
Persia to the degree that the 'bronze-headed spear' does for Greece.

Hence at the start of the tragedy Dareios, stern and dignified, is called 'lord of the bow' (*Persai* 55–57), while at its end Xerxes, petulant and ineffective, has lost his bow and his quiver is empty (*Persai* 1018–1023). We must remember, of course, that the bow was not a usual Greek weapon. The Greeks themselves used a self-bow made of a single flexible wooden staff, but Cretan archers, often hired as mercenaries, used a composite bow, as did Scythian archers, who, if not in Persian service, were also employed at this time by Greek states, especially Athens.

The composite bow consisted of a wooden core onto which was laminated sinew (front) and horn (back). The elasticity of the sinew meant that when the bow was drawn it stretched and was put under tension. By contrast, the strips of horn were compressed. By exploiting their mechanical properties, both materials thus reacted to propel the bowstring. This type of bow was very difficult to string and required the use of both legs and arms. Scythian arrows were short with small heads, much like those of the Persians, but in his capacious *gorytos* the archer carried both his bow and a great many diminutive arrows. Herodotos (4.64.3) says human skin, from enemy limbs, was favoured for covering the *gorytos* because of its whiteness. When firing, the Scythians (and Persians) employed the Mediterranean release, a method by which only the bowstring is drawn. With this firing technique the bowstring is drawn back to the chin or chest by the tips of three fingers with the arrow lightly held like a cigarette, if held at all, between the first and second fingers. The fourth finger and thumb are not used. In this they contrasted with the normal Greek practice, which was to pinch the arrow between thumb and forefinger, a weak grip that meant that Greeks were unable to draw the powerful composite bows of the Scythians or Persians.

This may in part explain why the full value of archers was only gradually appreciated in Greece towards the end of the Peloponnesian War. In Homer's *Iliad* the bow is only used by a couple of heroes on

Glazed ceramic bricks (London, British Museum) from the old palace of Dareios, Sousa (c. 500 BC). This panel shows a member of the Immortals, one of the Ten Thousand elite bodyguards of the Great King. This professional soldier is shown here as he would appear in peacetime, that is, in Persian ceremonial dress. (Author's collection)

either side, and there is some suggestion in later literature that archers were generally despised. Certainly 'spindles' (*atraktoi*, i.e. arrows) were regarded by the Spartans as the weapons of the womanly and weak, in contrast to the spear and shield of the face-to-face, toe-to-toe hoplite warrior. There was something entirely unfair about the idea that a man could kill from afar without danger to himself, an act naturally more suited for barbarian foreigners than the Greeks themselves.

For protection the Persian foot soldier relied on his lightweight, wicker shield. This was usually fashioned out of canes threaded through a wet sheet of rawhide, and when hardened the combined virtues of the two materials employed made a shield capable of stopping arrows. The shield was both small and crescent shaped with upturned points (Gr. *pélte*), or large and rectangular (OP *spara*). The latter, which in effect was like a medieval pavise, would be planted in the ground, thereby allowing the archer to discharge his arrows from behind it in relative safety. Some troops carried a figure-of-eight-shaped shield (Gr. *gerrhon*), that is, oval with circular segments cut out of the sides, while the Gandharans carried round shields (OP *taka*) not dissimilar to the *aspis* of Greek hoplites. A few Persians wore metal helmets, but only the Egyptians and the Mesopotamian contingents wore armour for body protection, which could be little more than a leather corselet. But then the Persians virtually settled many of their battles from a distance.

The Persians relied on arrow fire to shred the opposition, and so with their massed deployment and rapid rate of fire – having their quivers hanging at their side at waist level afforded them to do this – would blanket the opposition. It is the Spartan Dienekes' bravura remark at Thermopylae, as recorded by Herodotos, which probably gives us our best impression of Persian archery. One of the Trachinians, presumably unfriendly to the Spartans for choosing his country to fight in, told him:

> 'Such was the number of the barbarians, that when they shot forth their arrows the sun would be darkened by their multitude'. Dienekes, not at all frightened at these words, but making light of the Median numbers, answered, 'Our Trachinian friend brings us excellent tidings. If the Medes darken the sun, we shall have our fight in the shade'.
>
> Herodotos 7.226

This description of blotting out the sun suggests the Persians were shooting at long range with a parabolic trajectory. As we shall see, even despite the volume of arrows, the heavily armoured Spartans were able to shield themselves from the worst of it, and the Persians lightweight arrows were not able to penetrate their body armour or shields.

The Immortals

One corps of the *spada* consisted of 10,000 elite foot soldiers, the Immortals (Gr. *Athanatoi*, cf. OP *Amrtaka*, followers) as the Greeks called them, because they liked to believe, falsely, that their 'number was at no time either greater or less than ten thousand' (Herodotos 7.83.1). This superbly trained unit was mostly ethnic Persian though closely related Medes from northern Iran and Elamites from southern Iran are also known to have been members. These had variegated costumes adapted from the Elamite court dress – a fluted pillbox type of hat (although headgear varied), a calf-length tunic over tight-fitting trousers, and strapped soft shoes – and acted as the Great King's guard both in peace and war.

The standard campaign dress, on the other hand, is believed to have been the more practical outfit of Median style, namely a long-sleeved, knee-length, loose-fitting tunic, a pair of close-fitting trousers, and soft leather boots (a refinement unknown to the Greek hoplite). Headgear consisted of the traditional Persian *tiara*, a soft cloth hood with three lappets, two of which could be drawn across the face to keep out wind and dust. In the words of Herodotos, 'of these, one thousand carried spears with golden pomegranates at the lower end instead of spikes; and these encircled the other nine thousand, who bore on their spears pomegranates of silver' (7.41.2). At Thermopylae these crack troops were led by Hydarnes, son of Hydarnes, one of the six noble Persians who had helped Dareios to take the throne.

In addition, there was an elite within an elite, the unit of foot soldiers made up of 'one thousand spearmen, the noblest and bravest of the Persians' (Herodotos 7.41.1). These formed a personal bodyguard, the hand-picked warriors that followed close after the Great King. Officially known as the 'King's spear-bearers' (OP *Arštibara*), their short spears were distinctively knobbed with golden apples, from which they gained the nickname the 'apple-bearers' (Gr. *melophoroi*). As a prince of the cadet branch of the Achaemenidae, Dareios served in this illustrious guard of spearmen during Kambyses' Egyptian campaign (Herodotos 3.139.2). It seems that the King's spear-bearers with their famed apple-butted spears were formed from the Persian nobility, while the Immortals were from the pick of Persian, Median and Elamite commoners. Their commander was the *hazarapatiš* of the empire, who, as the officer next to the Great King, possessed vast political power. Cavalry units of the same type and strength (10,000 and 1,000) are also attested as part of the *spada* (Herodotos 7.41).

The Persian cavalry

The cavalry had been instrumental in conquering subject lands, and it retained its importance to the last days of the Achaemenid empire. It was Kyros who had organized and financed the first Persian cavalry, using booty and land gained in campaigns in the west. To establish the kingdom's horsepower he bestowed land to Persians known as 'equals', and then required them to use this land to support the cost of cavalry from then on. For instance, he presented to a certain Pytharchos, a Greek name, seven cities in northern Anatolia (*FGrHist* 472 F6). The honorary title of *Huvaka* (kinsman) was given to 15,000 Persian nobles, and Kyros went so far as to require this cadre of Persian elites to ride everywhere and made it a disgrace for them to be seen on foot. The elite horsemen, 'a thousand strong' (Herodotos 8.113.2), were undoubtedly drawn from the *Huvaka*. The first Persian cavalry were probably modelled after the excellent cavalry of the neighbouring Medes.

Media, with its wide skies and lush plains, was commonly noted for a breed of dun and grey horses that grazed there, the so-called Nisaean horses renowned for their speed and endurance. It is said that the Persians had brought the rich 'Median grass', what we know as lucerne or alfalfa, with them into Greece in 490 BC with Datis' expeditionary

Detail of a brick panel (Paris, musée du Louvre) showing an Immortal bejewelled with a golden earring, while his immaculately coiffed, curled hairstyle is adorned with a simple fillet of twisted gold. Yet the Immortal was no palace dandy; on the contrary, he was a disciplined, highly motivated and professional soldier. (Esther Carré)

force (Pliny *Naturalis historia* 18.144). Seeds probably came in with their cavalry's fodder, and this fine 'blue grass' from the horse studs back in Media then became a food crop for horses on rich Greek soil.

The Persian horseman was equipped more or less like the foot soldier (Herodotos 7.86.1), although he carried two cornel-wood javelins (Gr. *palta*), 1.5 to 1.8m in length and tipped with bronze or iron heads. One *palton* would be thrown, the second could be thrown or used to thrust, Xenophon explicitly says (*Peri Hippikes* 12.12) it was a better thrusting weapon than the flimsy Greek cavalry spears. Instead of the traditional *tiara* some horsemen wore metal helmets, usually of bronze and pot shaped. Body armour could be worn, such as padded linen corselets made of two layers of linen, quilted and stuffed with cotton wool. Padded linen might not have given as much protection as bronze, but it was certainly lighter and more comfortable to wear. Though armour made from metal (iron or bronze) or horn scales was ideal, non-metallic armour seems to have been quite common.

A Babylonian document, written in Akkadian and dated to the second regnal year of Dareios II (422 BC), lists the requirements of a horseman as follows:

> *A horse along with its groom, harness, and an iron caparison, and a helmet, leather corselet, shield, 120 arrows, a mace of iron, two iron-headed javelins and ration money.*

Murašû Archive BE 10 61

Persian cavalry never seemed to fully adopt the use of shields during the Achaemenid period. Light shields of cane and rawhide first appeared around 450 BC, and it is thought Scythians, who carried a smaller elongated version of the *spara* for cavalry use, employed as mercenaries by the Persians first introduced their use. This is based on the appearance of Attic red figure pottery images showing mounted Persian-style figures carrying shields at this time.

A detail from the Alexander Sarcophagus (Istanbul, Arkeoloji Müzesi, 370 T), Royal Necropolis Sidon, showing an unshielded Persian horseman, who wears the usual Median costume and Persian *tiara*. Persian clothing generally was brightly coloured and embroidered with squares, lozenges, circles or rosettes, though no doubt the poorer men wore fewer and duller hues. (Esther Carré)

Persian horsemen rode without stirrups or rigid leather saddles, at most sitting on a padded horse blanket, and their horses were not even shod, although the dry climate helped to toughen hoofs. Yet the Persians were skilled in both skirmish and close-quarter fighting. When skirmishing, small independent bands would ride along the front of the opposition discharging volleys of javelins or arrows, then wheel away only to shoot at their foe as they retreated ('scoot and shoot'). When engaging in close-quarter fighting, horsemen clearly did not attempt to ride the opposition down, but attacked exposed flanks and rears. Cavalry of the day – indeed, until comparatively modern times – were not given to charging into unbroken foot formations.

Levies

Apart from the standing army, levies were raised from subject peoples when the need arose, and it took a long time, sometimes years, to muster a grand army. By the time Xerxes sought to annexe mainland Greece, the empire stretched from the Indus in the east to the Aegean in the west, and from the River Iaxartes (Syr-Darya) in the north to the First Cataract on the Nile in the south. A grand army, therefore, could easily reflect the size and varied population of the empire.

A fragmentary statue (Athens, Acropolis Museum, 602) of a Scythian horse-archer (c. 520 BC). The Scythians were among the earliest of a long line of nomadic herders who migrated west from central Asia. In Athens, under the Peisistratrid tyrants, Scythians served as mercenaries, and later, under the democratic regime, were employed as policemen. (Author's collection)

Herodotos provides us with our fullest list for such an army (although we should ignore the figures), namely that of the Greek expedition of Xerxes. Although most of these exotic and colourful contingents are not heard of again, there is no valid reason to doubt the accuracy of his description of the army review at Doriskos. Herodotos certainly researched this catalogue (7.61–87) with great thoroughness, and it seems likely that he was using an official Persian document promulgated by Xerxes himself. He lists 45 peoples, including Indians and Arabs armed with their native bows, organized into six broad ethnic corps and under 29 different commands.

The empire was divided into satrapies, each ruled by the Great King's appointed governor or satrap (OP *xšacapāvan*, literally 'protector of the realm'), whose number varied from 20 to 29 at different periods of Dareios' reign. Herodotos (3.89.1), speaking probably of the earlier part of the reign, mentions 20. An inscription (Fornara 34), written in Old Persian and displayed on the south retaining wall of the royal palace at Persepolis, enumerates 23 lands of the empire, and the trilingual inscription on Dareios' rock-cut tomb at Naqš-e Rustam, the burial site of the early Great Kings, just north of Persepolis, lists 29 lands. As viceroy, representing the Great King, a satrap levied and collected taxes (in cash or in kind), administered the king's justice, built and maintained royal roads suitable for horses, organized and sustained a fast courier service, and provided musters for grand armies and often commanded them. As royal appointees, they tended to be members of the ruling dynasty by birth or marriage.

Over and above the *levée-en-masse*, there were also many Persian garrisons in important centres of the empire, and satraps also had their bodyguards or *arštibara*, but these could not be depleted to form a grand

43

army on short notice because the danger of revolt was always present. Hill tribesmen nominally subject to the Great King but in practice independent, especially from eastern Iran and beyond, were more readily available and could be hired to fight for the occasion. Satrapal levies and tribal mercenaries were summoned to a recruiting station (OP *handaisa*) where they were marshalled and reviewed.

Statistics were not a strongpoint of our ancient sources, and 'barbarian' armies have a way of growing with gusto in the recounting of campaign tales. Thus, the size of a grand army was never as large as the Greeks exaggeratedly claim: the picturesque image offered by Herodotos (7.21.2, 187.2, 196.2) is that of the streams and rivers of Greece being drunk dry by the Persian hordes. Careful examination of topography, logistics (especially the essential matter of water supply), organization of the *spada*, and official battle orders enable historians to arrive at reasonable figures for Persian forces. Thus Xerxes' 1,700,000 fighting men that crossed the Hellespont (Herodotos 7.60.1) are whittled down to 60,000–70,000 troops, including about 10,000 horsemen, to which can be added 10,000–20,000 for Thracian and Greek allies picked up en route (Lazenby 1993: 92). Similarly, the 1,200,000-strong royal army of Artaxerxes II Mnemon at Cunaxa (Xenophon *Anabasis* 1.7.11) was in reality no more than 60,000 (Anderson 1974: 100).

Tactics

Before battle, a council of war was held and plans of action discussed. The line of battle was usually drawn up as follows: the foot soldiers were stationed in the centre, flanked by cavalry and supported by lightly armed troops. Centrally positioned and surrounded by his household troops, the commander-in-chief observed the battle lines and directed the action from an elevated point, both the safest and most logical position whence to issue orders. Greek historians obviously made much of the obvious dissimilarity. We only have to imagine Xerxes at Thermopylae, for instance, perched on a high-backed throne overlooking the killing ground, while Leonidas, like some Homeric warrior chieftain, fights down in the dust alongside his troops.

When the battle was joined the soldiers dressed ranks, plucked their first arrows and eyed the opposition. At the edge of bow range, 200m or thereabouts, the soldiers began to flex their weapons. Before the gap narrowed between the armies, the aim was to throw the enemy lines into confusion with crippling arrows. The effective killing range of the Persian bow was around 100m. Then the soldiers, drawing spear and battleaxe, moved in, supported by cavalry attacking the flanks. The Persians tended to be cautious and methodical, and their fighting style was thus essentially defensive. The key tactic was to gather their foot soldiers in close formation behind their pavises. From afar, they would then pelt the enemy with a rainstorm of arrows. Cavalry would charge in and harass the enemy with javelins or arrows. Whoever was left was often routed by this time, or met the points of Persian spears.

These tactics worked well on the broad plains of Asia against other Asiatic armies, but failed against Greek hoplites. Unless released directly at close range, the arrows were simply stopped by the body armour and the *aspis* of the hoplites, and once the hand-to-hand combat began, no amount of personal bravery could compensate for the Persians' lack of body armour and their inferior shock weapons. Indeed, even the imperial elite, the Immortals, were armed with a spear that was shorter than that wielded by the hoplites (Herodotos 7.211.2). At the battle of Plataia, for instance, a fierce hand-to-hand combat raged between the Persian and the Greek foot soldiers. In the words of Herodotos:

An Attic red figure amphora (Paris, musée du Louvre, G 106), attributed to the artist Euphronios (*c.* 510–500 BC). This detail shows a Scythian warrior wielding a *sagaris*, the slender battleaxe adopted by the Persians, and a *gorytos*, the combination quiver-holder and bow-case that was a characteristic of the mobile cultures of the steppe. (Esther Carré)

> [The Persians] many times seized hold of the Greek spears and broke them; for in boldness and warlike spirit the Persians were not a whit inferior to the Greeks; but they were unarmoured, untrained, and far below the enemy in respect of skill in arms. Sometimes singly, sometimes in bodies of ten, now fewer and now more in number, they dashed forward upon the Spartan ranks, and so perished.
>
> Herodotos 9.62.3

He also stresses that they were 'without protective clothing' (*gymnetes*, literally 'naked', 9.63.2), compared with Greek hoplites.

Thus, it was vital for the Persians to prevent the mêlée desired by the hoplite phalanx, and either to get the Greeks to stand and receive a barrage of arrows or bring them to a halt within effective firing range. Once the Greeks closed the advantage was with them, as the Persians were ill equipped and, more importantly, they lacked the cohesion to stand toe-to-toe with hoplites. Yet the Greeks were intrinsically no smarter or braver than the Persians, and if the latter attained the tactical conditions they desired, as they had done at Malēne, victory for them was assured. The hoplite phalanx was a simple instrument compared with the flexible Persian army, and, Marathon notwithstanding, the Greeks had yet to stand their ground against the Persians.

Medes and Persians

In the imagination of most Greek writers the barbarians *par excellence*, the quintessential 'other', were the Persians. Yet they typically confused the Persians and their near-relatives the Medes, using the name Mede (*Medos*) and Persian (*Persa*) in a general sense as synonymous terms. For example, the epitaph of the tragedian Aischylos, referring to his feat at the battle of Marathon, speaks of 'the long-haired Mede' as being a witness to those martial deeds. Persians were of the same *ethnos* as the Medes, that is, Iranian, and they were alike in religion and very akin in language. The Persian empire was in reality a joint kingdom of the Medes and Persians, but the origins of Kyros' creation of the Achaemenid dynasty lay in reversing the traditional political relationship between them. From now on the Persians of southern Iran were to be on the conductor's podium, and the Medes of northern Iran were to play second fiddle.

The Medo-Persian was an unusual product for an Asiatic soil. He was an Asian apart. Like the Greeks, the Asiatic of the time had a natural tendency towards polytheism. However, with the Persian monotheism was the set religion of the race. It had a legendary origin in the dualist teachings of the reforming prophet Zarathustra (or Zoroaster, as he is better known from the Latin), who said that Ahura Mazda was the one god. There were other objects of worship – stars, the sun, the moon, and fire, marvellous and incomprehensible creations of Ahura Mazda, the Wise Lord – but he was god alone. As the supreme deity of light and truth, his cult was promoted as a political tool, especially by Dareios. The new empire with which the Greeks had been brought into contact was not a mere aggregation of barbarism, but a highly organized piece of machinery controlled by people who were as sophisticated, if not more so, as the Greeks themselves.

An Attic red figure amphora (Paris, musée du Louvre, G 46), attributed to the artist Nikoxénos (c. 500 BC). This detail shows a hoplite departing for battle accompanied by a Scythian. Wearing a distinctive pointed hat, sat upright on his head, the warrior carries a *gorytos*, which houses his bow and arrows, and *sagaris*. (Esther Carré)

OPPOSING PLANS

The Persian Wars are the first in European history that we can really reconstruct, mainly because of the valiant efforts of Herodotos – the other evidence being comparatively negligible – who held the conflict between East and West as the key to all history. Yet his accounts do seem rather naive and full of colourful anecdotes and long digressions, both literary and personal. Moreover we find hardly any analysis on troop types, weaponry, logistics, or even staff matters. There is almost nothing about strategy and tactics, and the little there is seems absurd to us. For instance, any mention of tactics comes in the form of long-winded speeches from the mouths of generals and admirals just prior to an engagement. These speeches seem simplistic in technical detail and, what is more frustrating, are not authentic as they are constructed from general traditions of what happened rather than why it happened.

To be more charitable to Herodotos we should remember that a historian is only as good as his sources, and for events prior to 480 BC most of his evidence came from hearsay, while those after that date are from eyewitness accounts. Of course these eyewitnesses, both Greek and Persian, would have been the lesser soldiers who took part in the battles and not the generals and admirals, long dead by the time of his research. Besides the more mundane, these men were obviously not in the know about military matters and, therefore, his accounts of the discussions in the Greek and Persian councils of war must be treated with caution.

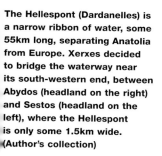

The Hellespont (Dardanelles) is a narrow ribbon of water, some 55km long, separating Anatolia from Europe. Xerxes decided to bridge the waterway near its south-western end, between Abydos (headland on the right) and Sestos (headland on the left), where the Hellespont is only some 1.5km wide. (Author's collection)

Some scholars argue, and even accuse, Herodotos of incompetence in matters military. The usual argument is that Herodotos was not a military man and thus did not understand what made generals and admirals 'tick'. Yet these generals (*stratēgoi*) and admirals (*nauarchoi*) were not the most skilled men of their day. An Athenian *stratēgos*, for instance, was elected to his office and could command, and often did, both on land and sea. Indeed, we could hardly regard Themistokles, who had never commanded a fleet prior to Artemision, as an expert in warfare; although he was a man from outside the charmed circle of Athenian blue-blooded aristocracy, he owed his position to circumstances of birth and wealth. Ancient warfare is of a different order to that of modern warfare. Apart from the odd military manual (Xenophon's *Kyropaideia* for instance) there was no formal training or *Kriegsakademien*, and the two greatest generals of antiquity, Alexander and Hannibal, learnt their trade at their fathers' knees. At the end of the day, therefore, we must believe Herodotos' facts, but we must question his explanations of why certain things happened.

THE GREEK PLAN

Resistance in mainland Greece centred on Sparta and its Peloponnesian allies, but Athens also joined the alliance against Persia – what modern commentators usually call the Hellenic League – with a scattering of other states in central Greece and nearby islands. At first other states as far north as Thessaly were willing to fight, and following an appeal from the Thessalians, an expedition of 10,000 hoplites was sent to hold the Vale of Tempē (Témbi) near Mount Olympos. This army was reinforced by Thessalian horsemen on arrival, but quickly withdrew after a warning of the size of Xerxes' forces and realizing that Tempē could be turned, leaving the Thessalians with no alternative but to 'medize' (*medizein*), that is, to submit to the Great King. It was then decided to hold Thermopylae, while stationing the Hellenic League fleet off Artemision, some 40 nautical miles to the east on the northern coast of Euboia (Evvía), the long fish-like island that guards the coast of Attica. Here for three days the Greeks more than held their own against the Persians, although the losses they sustained and the fall of Thermopylae eventually compelled withdrawal.

The whole issue of Greek strategy is complicated by the Troizen Decree, a document inscribed on a marble stele (monument stone) with third-century lettering. In 1959 Jameson rediscovered the decree at the back of a café in Troizen, the Peloponnesian town reputedly the birthplace of the legendary Theseus of Athens. Much to the delight of the academic world, the inscription was quickly published (Jameson 1960). Obviously the authenticity of this decree is fiercely contested by scholars, and there are those, such as Lazenby (1993: 102–104), who believe it to be a patriotic fabrication of the fourth century BC, put in its final form in the third, rather than a true copy of an official Athenian decree of 481/480 BC.

The inscription (Fornara 55), also known as the Themistokles Decree from the name of the man who apparently moved its passage through the Athenian assembly, talks of the early evacuation of Attica and the mobilization of the fleet with the intention of halting the Persians at the Isthmus of Corinth, gateway to the Peloponnese, and not at Thermopylae and Artemision; the Athenians originally planned to send only half their navy north at once, keeping the other 100 triremes in reserve round Salamis and Attica. If this is all accurate, which would have been decided before the Persians actually invaded, then we could reasonably argue that the Greeks were thinking ahead. But in Herodotos' version of events the Greeks do no such thing. On the contrary, they are playing by ear rather than following a master plan.

As Burn (1984: 367–68) points out, the number of ten hoplites only, aged between 20 and 30, as marines (*epibatai*) gives rise to a certain amount of uneasiness. The number is consistent with what Herodotos (7.185.1, 8.17) appears to have thought was the normal complement of Greek warships at this time, but both he and the decree are probably anachronistic here. It was this number that the swift Athenian triremes of the Peloponnesian War, which manoeuvred for an attack with the ram, carried (Thucydides 2.23.2, 3.94.1, 95.2), but it seems that this number must have represented a reduction since earlier times. Thucydides, on the sea-fight between Corinth and Corcyra off Sybota (433 BC), speaks of 'many hoplites, javelin throwers and archers on the decks' as characteristic of 'the old-fashioned kind' (1.49.1).

Actually we are reminded of the Chiot triremes at Lade (494 BC), which each carried 40 picked hoplites who served as *epibatai* (Herodotos 6.15.2). It seems certain that, in the ships of his novel, mass-produced navy with which he was so anxious to give battle in narrow waters, Themistokles must have planned to carry many more hoplites than ten per ship. There were certainly no Athenian hoplites at Thermopylae as there had been earlier at Tempē, and it cannot be imagined that those over 30 years of age simply stayed in Attica when the fleet went north.

Two serious questions are provoked by Herodotos' narrative of Thermopylae: first, why did Leonidas have so few men under his command? And, second, what actually happened on that final, fateful day? The question of the final catastrophe will be dealt with later. As to the size of Leonidas' army, Herodotos repeatedly says (7.203.1, 206.2, 208, 8.40) that this force was only an advanced guard (*prodromoi*, literally 'fore-runners') of a much larger army; in other words, despite some modern theories to the contrary, Thermopylae was intended to be an 'all-out effort'. Yet the fall of Thermopylae was, to the Greeks at least, unexpectedly swift (Herodotos 7.206.2) and the Athenians at Artemision, for instance, where the bulk of their hoplites were serving as marines, believed that the main Peloponnesian land force would eventually concentrate in central Greece. Sparta alone, for example, with only ten triremes at Artemision (Herodotos 8.1.2), could clearly have dispatched many more hoplites to Thermopylae, however many marines we estimate each of its ships carried. Sparta was said by Herodotos (7.234.2) to have had at least 8,000 adult male citizen warriors at this time.

The excuse given for delaying the dispatching of reinforcements north was the celebration of the Doric festival of Apollo Karneia and the panhellenic Olympic Games (Herodotos 7.206.1). The feast of Apollo Karneia, which occurred at the third moon after the summer solstice, was the most sacred part of a sacred month when no Dorian might

The northern entrance to the Persian canal on the Mount Athos peninsula was located at what is now the village of Nea Rōda, which lies in the dip, seen centre left. The Persians built protective moles at either end, and those at this end of the canal can be made out just beyond the village. On the horizon is Cape Arapis. (Author's collection)

march to war, and no one in antiquity ever doubted such religious scruples (Thucydides 5.54, 76, Plato *Laws* 698E, Xenophon *Hellenika* 4.7.2). And so it was that the Spartans had not stood beside the Athenians when they had won their victory at Marathon. After the full moon 2,000 Spartan hoplites had left for Attica and arrived after only three days, but just too late. They demanded to see the dead Persians, and, having done so, and praised the work of the Athenians, they tramped home again (Herodotos 6.106.3, 120). The reason given by the Spartans for not going to Thermopylae in full strength, on the basis of the Marathon evidence alone, will be seen as perfectly genuine.

The limited number of non-Dorian Peloponnesians is also accounted for by a religious commitment, although in their case it was the quadrennial Olympic festival in honour of the god Zeus that kept many of them away. Every four years three sacred heralds set out from Olympia to visit every corner of the Greek world proclaiming a sacred truce, affording safe passage through any state for travellers to and from the festival. All Greeks were invited to attend the sacred event at the sanctuary of Zeus at Olympia, the central day of which always coincided with either the second or the third moon after the summer solstice. As Greek states tended to fight against rather than alongside one another, hence the sacred truce to enforce amity, these panhellenic gatherings were vital to Greek ethnicity. At Olympia spectators and participants from Greek states throughout the Mediterranean shared a common culture in which religious piety and enthusiasm for sport were of pivotal importance.

Only free, male Greeks could compete in the games, and an athletic victory was thought to bring a winner closer to the gods themselves. As the Olympic contestants performed in his sanctuary, to win was attributed to the inspiration and favour of Zeus himself. Often a victor was actually said to appear god-like himself. To put this into the context of that other major Greek event of 480 BC, the Olympic Games were in the final stages of preparation even as Leonidas and his minuscule force were preparing to sacrifice themselves. A few days later, while the Persians were torching Athens, the games took place in the sanctuary at

Olympia. The athletes, like the crowd as a whole, came from all over Greece, although no Spartans or Athenians are known to have competed while their fellow citizens were dying at Persian hands.

Of course, modern sceptics can easily suggest a less noble reason, which is that the Peloponnesian states were reluctant to commit their manpower to the defence of central mainland Greece. Yet the strategy of the Hellenic League was bound to be a compromise between stopping Xerxes as far north as possible, thus allowing as many Greek states to join in the resistance as could do so, and the natural desire to defend one's own territory. It must be remembered that in this period of Greek history there was little or no ethnic patriotism. A man belonged to his *polis* long before he had any concept of Hellas or of all mainland Greeks forming a coherent nation. The *poleis* functioned independently of each other, forming alliances, trading, and going to war just like separate nations. This state of affairs meant that Thermopylae was fated to be a classic compromise, and as normal with compromises it was doomed to failure.

To the Greeks, long-term strategy and planning were a mystery in 480 BC, which is clearly apparent when we consider that they had never fought a war on such a large scale before, unlike the Persians. Those 10,000 hoplites despatched to the riverine pass of Tempē probably represented, in the Greek generals' minds, a large army. We are also dealing with states whose military experience was usually confined to cross-border incursions not full-scale invasions, Greeks at that time rarely engaging in battle outside their local known territory. Nevertheless, the members of the Hellenic League first met at the Isthmus of Corinth in the autumn of 481 BC to reconcile their differences, send out spies, and secure help elsewhere. A second conference was convened in the spring of the following year when a delegation from Thessaly asked for military aid, hence the 10,000 hoplites ordered to the Vale of Tempē.

If there had been no Thessalian appeal then the Greeks would have probably made their stand at Thermopylae, and Herodotos does in fact hint at this. Besides, if guarded by a sufficient number of troops, it was the natural place to stop an invader entering Greece from the north: the Greeks held Thermopylae again against Brennus and his Gauls (279 BC); Antiochos the Great met the Romans here (191 BC); and New Zealand forces held the pass in a rearguard action against the Wehrmacht (1941), only to be dislodged by Stuka dive-bombers.

Of course, Leonidas did eventually stand here in the high summer of 480 BC, with a small force representing a wavering grouping of anti-Persian Greeks – 300 Spartans, 2,120 Arcadians, 400 Corinthians, 200 from Phleious, 80 from Mycenae (all Peloponnesians); 700 Thespians and 400 Thebans (representing Boiotia); and from the local Greek people most directly affected, 1,000 Phokians and the full force of the Opountian Lokrians (Herodotos 7.202–203.1), estimated by Diodoros (11.4.7) at 1,000 men. Each contingent served under its own *stratēgos*.

In his version of the battle Herodotos also implies (7.229.1) that there was one helot in attendance on each Spartiate at Thermopylae. Likewise it would be surprising if there were no *perioikoi* (the inhabitants of the villages around Sparta, literally 'those who dwell around') present too, and it could be argued that the *perioikoi* fielded the same number of troops as the Spartans, as they were to do the following year at Plataia

The canal the Persians dug across the isthmus on the Mount Athos peninsula for passage of the invasion fleet took three years to complete. In this aerial shot of the peninsula, taken looking south-east towards Mount Athos, the northern entrance can be made out on the left, halfway up. (Author's collection)

(Herodotos 9.11.3). Even though they lacked citizen rights, the *perioikoi* were expected to fight in the Spartan army. The Athenian Isokrates later speaks (4.90, 6.99) of 1,000 Lakedaimonians in all marching to Thermopylae, which looks like a conveniently round number for the Spartans, *perioikoi* and helots with Leonidas. This would bring the total of 3,100 Peloponnesians given by Herodotos into line with the war-memorial inscription he quotes (7.228.1), and which claims that 4,000 men from the Peloponnese fought at Thermopylae.

Despite the Karneia imposing a taboo upon Spartans' fighting, it is possible that Sparta recognized the absolute necessity of sending some troops north to defend the pass. Leonidas himself chose the Three Hundred so that any losses should not extinguish any Spartan line. Lazenby (1985: 54–55) suggests that this selection was done by lot, thereby putting the onus on the Gods to decide who was to go, whilst Leonidas himself may have been held to be exempt from the taboo because he was beyond military age, having passed his 60th birthday.

THE PERSIAN PLAN

We know almost nothing about the Persian strategy apart from the obvious, that is, Xerxes' invasion was not just to punish Athens but an all-out attempt to conquer the whole of mainland Greece. For Herodotos it all boils down to the personal foibles of a sacrilegious autocrat, Xerxes himself, and, although we should not dismiss this out of hand, we should explore more rational reasons too.

Persia was vast and rich, but Greece was small and poor; it had little to offer the Great King who, after all, was the richest man on earth. Yet the immeasurable perimeter of his polyglot realm was vulnerable. The one obvious advantage of conquering rock-strewn Greece that might have occurred to the Persian high command was the belief that their empire would never really be secure when there was a definite possibility of revolt, backed up by the Greek mainland, of the Greek states in Aegean Anatolia. A second possibility is tied up with the circumstances that led to Xerxes' elevation to the throne, which suggests that he and his supporters needed to reinforce their position through conquest and, of course, glory. However, beyond that things are not at all clear.

The Persians did not appreciate the extent to which the Greeks were to unite, so the high command may have reasoned that the invasion was to be an exercise in taking each Greek state in turn, much as they had done during the mopping-up operations that followed the collapse of the Ionian revolt. They did not plan in some detail, therefore, the invasion as a whole, apart from the close co-operation between the fleet and the army. The fleet was detailed to bypass Greek positions on land, a fact hinted at in a conversation recorded by Herodotos, which took place after the battle at Thermopylae, between Xerxes and Demaratos, or so he says. However, true or not, the erstwhile king of Sparta proposed that the Persian fleet should bypass the Isthmus of Corinth to harry Lakonia from the sea and thereby compel the Spartans to return home, but this stratagem was supposedly rejected by the Great King's brother, Achaemenes, commander of the fleet. Yet even if we do not believe that Herodotos is recording an actual debate, we can see that such stratagems by the Persian fleet existed.

Even though they had suffered defeat, the Marathon campaign had shown the Persians the feasibility of transporting men and horses by sea. In addition to this offensive role, however, the fleet took on a second one, which was, broadly speaking, defensive in nature. The Persians were not seamen, having acquired their navy through the conquest of seagoing people such as the Egyptians, Phoenicians and Asiatic Greeks. Nevertheless they were not slow to realize that the new navy of Athens, the ships that were ultimately to give it its empire, was quite capable of threatening their lines of communication across the Aegean or even raising a revolt behind their backs.

Finally, a third role for the fleet has been advanced by many modern commentators, namely that of supply and transport. This idea can be disputed because of the lack of evidence for such. In Herodotos there are only two passages relative to the issue of sea-borne supplies. The first one talks of the creation of supply dumps on land across Thrace, but supplied by sea to dump and not direct to the army. The second covers the great summer storm off Magnesia that wrecked the fleet (originally

The southern entrance to the Persian canal on the Mount Athos peninsula is now nothing more than a marsh. The isthmus has risen some 14m since the canal was cut, though a shallow depression still remains. The canal had a length of approximately 2.2km and was wide enough to allow two triremes to be rowed through it simultaneously. (Author's collection)

Strymōn, at Nine Ways, Thrace, site of the later Athenian colony of Amphipolis. This is the old road bridge, seen from what the British, fighting German and Bulgarian forces (1916–18), called St Catherine's Hill (Hill 164). It was somewhere here that the river was bridged by Persian engineers for Xerxes' army. (Author's collection)

1,207 triremes); 400 triremes destroyed and an uncountable number of merchantmen lost is Herodotos' estimate (7.190–191). In reply we can point out the fact that, even if we do not accept Herodotos' figures for the original size of the Persian fleet, there was in reality a very large body of fleet personnel who needed feeding at least once a day, if not twice, and thus these hulks may well have been carrying supplies to keep the fleet provisioned, not the army.

The clincher, however, is the fact that for several weeks in the early part of the invasion the fleet and army were operating as separate entities. The army had moved down to Thermopylae while the fleet held station off Artemision, and it was not until after these two engagements that the two came together. As for supplying the army, it was a fairly straightforward matter of food dumps, the supply column and, of course, stealing and extorting provisions from the locals, otherwise known as 'living off the land'.

THE CAMPAIGN BEGINS

In the autumn of 481 BC Xerxes, who was to lead the invasion in person, moved his grand army to Sardis in order to spend the winter there in training. The figures given by Herodotos are impossibly high. He claims the total manpower was 5,283,220 gathered from all over the empire (7.186.2), the infantry numbering 1,700,000 (7.60.1), as well as 300,000 from those Thracians and Greeks who had 'medized' (7.185.2), with the cavalry, apart from the camels and chariots, numbering 80,000 (7.87.1). Modern scholarship has rejected these numbers and has settled on 80,000 as a sober estimate of Xerxes' land forces, with the main fighting strength being Iranian troops, and the rest perhaps useful but token contingents from all the subject races.

Herodotos gives the size of the Persian fleet as 1,207 triremes (7.89–95, 184.1) with an addition of 120 ships from the Greeks of Thrace and its offshore islands (7.185.1). It seems possible that he is recording here the paper strength of the Persian navy and not the operation number of Xerxes' invasion fleet, although it is interesting to note that Aischylos (*Persai* 341–343), who was probably there, gives the same original figure – albeit for Salamis. As Lazenby points out, 'it is worth remembering that ships are much easier to count than men' (1993: 94). Be that as it may, the full complement of a trireme was 200 (Herodotos 7.184.1, 185.1, 8.17), of whom 170 were oarsmen. Persian triremes, again according to Herodotos (7.184.2), carried, apart from an unspecified

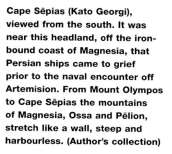

Cape Sēpias (Kato Georgi), viewed from the south. It was near this headland, off the iron-bound coast of Magnesia, that Persian ships came to grief prior to the naval encounter off Artemision. From Mount Olympos to Cape Sēpias the mountains of Magnesia, Ossa and Pēlion, stretch like a wall, steep and harbourless. (Author's collection)

Artemision took its name from a temple erected there to the goddess Artemis 'Facing the East' (*Prosēōia*): this epithet arose from the fact that it was here that ships took their departure eastwards across the Aegean. This is Cape Artemision, the northernmost tip of Evvía (Euboia), off which the sea fight took place. (Author's collection)

View of Aphetai (Platania), the legendary starting point of Jason and the Argonauts, just west of Cape Sēpias. The Persian fleet was too large for one harbour and so was spread out over several. Today a pleasant coastal resort, Platania itself consists of a series of small beaches separated by rocky promontories. (Author's collection)

number of native marines, 30 additional fighting men who were Persians, Medes or Scythians, the last of whom were highly valued for their archery skills. Every Persian ship was supplied by a Persian subject state, including Phoenicians, Egyptians, Carians, Cypriots and Greeks, among others. The non-seafaring Persians supplied only admirals and marines. The last were probably crowded onboard to ensure the loyalty of the ship's company and for that reason they were undoubtedly carried in battle.

Xerxes set out in the spring of 480 BC, crossing the Hellespont in early June and advancing west across Thrace and Macedonia, then south into central Greece. Herodotos says that the Great King, prior to crossing into Europe, 'sacrificed a thousand oxen to the Trojan Athena' (7.43). According to tradition, the Greeks themselves had invaded Asia nearly a thousand years before. Such are the long memories of the ancients. As we have already discussed, the Greeks intended to stop Xerxes at the valley of the River Peneios at Tempē, the main pass into Thessaly from Macedonia, but this position was abandoned before the crossing of the Hellespont. Returning to the Isthmus of Corinth, the Greeks debated where next to try to make a stand. The decision was to occupy the pass at Thermopylae with a force of around 7,000 hoplites under Leonidas. At the same time a fleet of 271 (later reinforced by 53) triremes and nine penteconters (50-oared galleys) sailed to Artemision on the northernmost spur of the island of Euboia under the nominal command of the Spartan admiral Eurybiades, son of Euryklides.

THE NAVAL BATTLE OF ARTEMISION

The Greeks were probably afraid that the Persians would turn their position at Thermopylae by the sea. Yet the station off Artemision was at least 40 nautical miles from Thermopylae, hence an eight-hour row there and an eight-hour row back if we are to assume that the cruising speed of a trireme was in the region of five knots. Effectively this meant there

The Peneios (Piniós), while providing an ample water supply, takes up so large a part of the Vale of Tempē (Témbi) that in a number of places there is no more space than some 27m through which an army can pass. However, there are other routes into Thessaly farther to the west. (Author's collection)

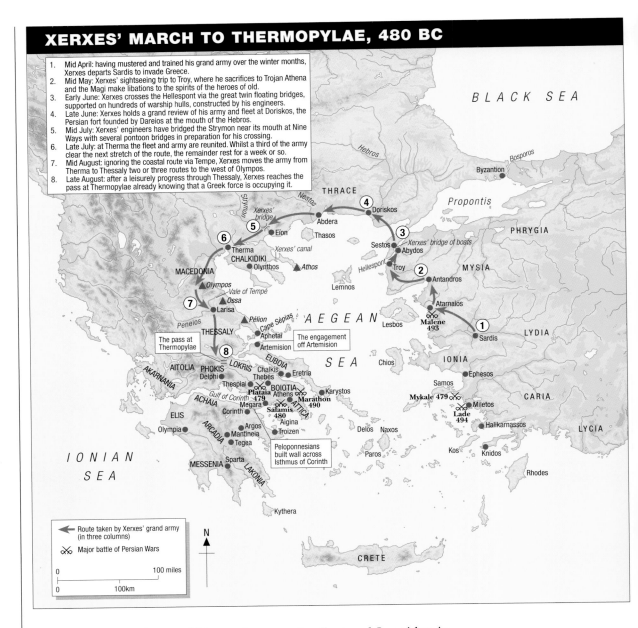

1. Mid April: having mustered and trained his grand army over the winter months, Xerxes departs Sardis to invade Greece.
2. Mid May: Xerxes' sightseeing trip to Troy, where he sacrifices to Trojan Athena and the Magi make libations to the spirits of the heroes of old.
3. Early June: Xerxes crosses the Hellespont via the great twin floating bridges, supported on hundreds of warship hulls, constructed by his engineers.
4. Late June: Xerxes holds a grand review of his army and fleet at Doriskos, the Persian fort founded by Dareios at the mouth of the Hebros.
5. Mid July: Xerxes' engineers have bridged the Strymon near its mouth at Nine Ways with several pontoon bridges in preparation for his crossing.
6. Late July: at Therma the fleet and army are reunited. Whilst a third of the army clear the next stretch of the route, the remainder rest for a week or so.
7. Mid August: ignoring the coastal route via Tempe, Xerxes moves the army from Therma to Thessaly two or three routes to the west of Olympos.
8. Late August: after a leisurely progress through Thessaly, Xerxes reaches the pass at Thermopylae already knowing that a Greek force is occupying it.

was a time delay of some 48 hours between the fleet and Leonidas: in other words, direct communications between the two Greek commands were non-existent. So why did the Greeks not position the fleet directly off Thermopylae?

The logistics required to support both fleet and army was beyond the capabilities of the area. The Greeks could have stationed their fleet at a number of more feasible locations closer to Thermopylae, but it seems nearness was not the only issue. Nor was the potential engagement site, since the straits between Artemision and the mainland are some 14km wide, and the heavily outnumbered Greeks would have preferred fighting in narrower waters. In truth we do not really know why the Greeks chose Artemision, but we can make a guess at various possibilities.

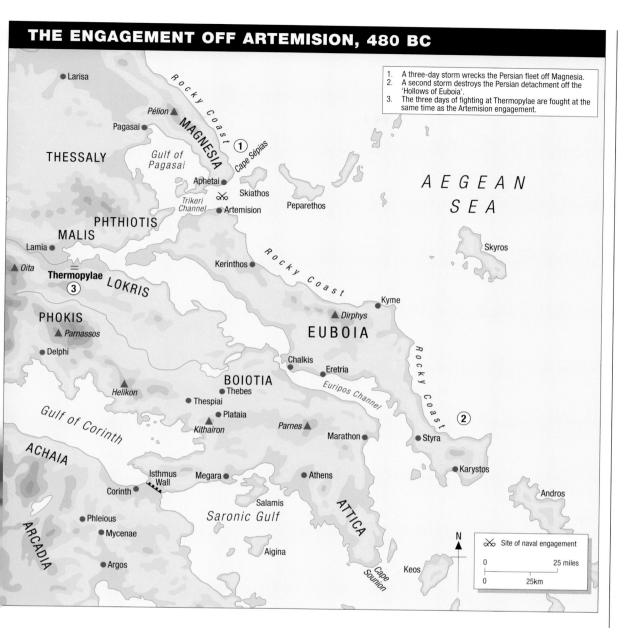

1. A three-day storm wrecks the Persian fleet off Magnesia.
2. A second storm destroys the Persian detachment off the 'Hollows of Euboia'.
3. The three days of fighting at Thermopylae are fought at the same time as the Artemision engagement.

Larisa

Rocky Coast

Pélion ▲
MAGNESIA
Pagasai ●

THESSALY

Gulf of Pagasai

Cape Sépias
①

Aphetai ●

Trikeri Channel

Skiathos

Artemision

Peparethos

AEGEAN SEA

PHTHIOTIS

MALIS

Lamia ●

Skyros

▲ Oita

Thermopylae
③

LOKRIS

Rocky Coast

Kerinthos ●

Kyme ●

PHOKIS

▲ Parnassos

▲ Dirphys

● Delphi

EUBOIA

Rocky Coast

Chalkis ●

Eretria ●

BOIOTIA

Helikon ▲

Euripos Channel

● Thebes

● Thespiai

● Plataia

Kithairon ▲

Parnes ▲

②

Gulf of Corinth

Marathon ●

Styra ●

ACHAIA

Isthmus Wall

Megara ●

Athens ●

Karystos ●

Corinth ●

Andros

● Phleious

Salamis

Saronic Gulf

ATTICA

● Mycenae

Aigina

N

✄ Site of naval engagement

ARCADIA

● Argos

Cape Sounion

Keos

0 — 25 miles
0 — 25km

By lying off the northern tip of Euboia the Greek fleet was preventing the Persians from sailing around the north of the island and thus down the western seaboard through the inland waterway between it and the mainland. The bleak eastern seaboard of Euboia was, and still is, a hostile stretch of water. Normally it is a windward shore that lacks safe havens, unlike the gentler western seaboard, and it is worth reminding ourselves of the 400 Persian triremes wrecked by a violent north-easterly storm off the iron-bound coast of Magnesia. Another possibility is that the Greeks feared, by not holding station off Euboia per se, that the island would be abandoned to the Persians – Eretria and Chalkis, the two leading states, were both members of the Hellenic League – who could then land troops at the northern end of the island, march south, and then make the short crossing over to Attica.

The Greek anchorage has been identified as the broad, open beach at Pévki, 10km west of Cape Artemision. West of Pévki the beaches stretch out in an almost unbroken chain along the north coast of Evvía (Euboia), and the Greek triremes would have ample space to beach in a single line. (Author's collection)

The actual naval engagement off Artemision is not fully described by Herodotos. The Persian fleet, now reduced by storm losses, was beached at Aphetai (Platanliá) just opposite Artemision some 16km to the north-east. On realization that the Greeks were nearby the Persians sent a force of 200 triremes southwards on a route east of Euboia to round the island and cut the enemy's line of retreat through the inner channel. Their intention was to offer battle as soon as they heard that it was cut. The Greeks, however, 'with the intention of testing Persian seamanship and tactics' (Herodotos 8.9), came out late in that first day so that the action should not last long. They appreciated that in a protracted engagement the overriding numbers of the Persian fleet would eventually tell. In response the Persian crews, who could hardly believe their eyes, quickly manned their ships confidently expecting an easy victory 'seeing that the Greek ships were few, while their own were many times more numerous and better sailing' (Herodotos 8.10.1), and encircled the Greek ships.

This was the naval tactic known as the *diekplous*, 'rowing through and out'. In this hazardous manoeuvre, a single trireme or, preferably, triremes in line abreast, rowed through a gap in the enemy line, and quickly came about to ram in side or stern. In response the Greeks changed formation from line abreast, in which they could have been outflanked in open water, and 'formed into a close circle, with bows outwards and sterns to the centre' (Herodotos 8.11.1), and succeeded in taking 30 vessels. Normally this defensive tactic was only employed by a slower, weaker fleet, but it is hard to imagine 271 triremes, the nominal strength of the Greek fleet on this day, forming a circle, which would have measured some 5km in circumference. Yet Herodotos does not actually use the word 'circle' (*kuklos*) in his narrative but employs the phraseology 'they drew their sterns together towards the middle', in other words a bow-shaped formation. Thus, they compelled the enemy to ram prow to prow, and, in the end, brought about a mêlée in which the speed and manoeuvrability of the enemy ships were of no advantage.

The following night a second summer storm, accompanied by torrential rain, drove the 200-ship force upon the rocks of the windswept and treacherous eastern coast, off what Herodotos calls 'the Hollows of Euboia' (8.13), and totally destroyed them. Next morning – likewise the second day of fighting at Thermopylae – news of the destruction of the Persian task force reached the Greek fleet, and shortly afterwards further Athenian reinforcements of 53 triremes arrived. Herodotos says almost nothing about the second day's fighting off Artemision. The Greeks again came out late in the day against some Cilician ships and 'having destroyed them, when night came, they sailed back to Artemision' (8.14.2).

Finally, on the third day, the frustrated Persian admirals, thinking of Xerxes' anger at those who failed him, put to sea first, arranging their ships in a sickle-shaped formation as the fleet rowed out from the coast of Magnesia. At first the Greeks made no move, but as the enemy approached the beach at Artemision they came out in full force, and took the initiative in attack. The Persian ships apparently fell back in some confusion, but did not break their line, and the two fleets separated after some bitter fighting and heavy casualties on both sides. The most formidable fighters that day were the heavily armed Egyptian marines. In Herodotos' catalogue of Persian forces they are described as wearing 'reticulated helmets and were armed with concave, broad-rimmed shields, boarding-spears, and heavy axes, and most of them also wore corselets and carried long knives' (7.89.2) – appropriate arms for close-quarter action aboard ship. By the end of the day they had carried five Greek triremes by boarding and taken them 'with their crews' (Herodotos 8.17).

That evening the Greeks heard the fate of Leonidas at Thermopylae and took the decision to withdraw southwards that very night, abandoning Euboia (and Attica) to the enemy. The contemporary Theban poet, Pindar, may have been right when he said that Artemision was 'where the sons of Athens laid the shining foundation-stone of freedom' (ap. Plutarch *Themistokles* 8.2), yet it was to be the heroic last stand at Thermopylae that would act as the major inspiration to the Greeks.

As this scale model (Edinburgh, Royal Museum, T 1980.31) demonstrates, a trireme, the principal warship of the period, was a sleek wooden vessel armed with a bronze-sheathed ram. It could be powered either by oar or sail, but in battle only oars were used, as speed and manoeuvrability were everything. (Author's collection)

THE BATTLE OF THERMOPYLAE

Rather than yield an inch at Thermopylae, Leonidas sacrificed his men's lives and his own. Tyrtaios (*fl. c.* 650 BC), favourite poet in Sparta, summed up the laconic ethos of the Spartans in his ode to the noble death in battle: 'So let each stand his ground firmly with his feet well set apart and bite his lip' (fr. 10 West). Yet the self-chosen and avoidable death of Leonidas marked the end, not the beginning, of the battle. Indeed, the Spartan king had chosen his terrain wisely and his tactics logically. He reasoned that in the defile of Thermopylae a small number of resolute men could hold off the Persian juggernaut. There is no reason to believe that Leonidas and his men thought that they were doomed, except perhaps on the morning of the final day. A contemporary of Tyrtaios, Archilochos, offers us a much better, and safer, analogy in his preference for the down-to-earth *stratēgos* 'set firm on his feet and full of guts' (fr. 114 West).

When Leonidas stood at Thermopylae there was only a narrow passage between the mountains on his left and the sea to his right. These mountains, the Kallidromos range, stretch in an east–west direction hugging the coast of the Malian Gulf, and at three points they came very close to the sea. Two of these points were even narrower, one to the east (East Gate) and one to the west (West Gate), than his chosen position (Middle Gate), which itself was barely 15m wide. Yet Leonidas eliminated them from his plan because in both of them the landward slopes, though steep, were far from sheer. He opted, therefore, for a slightly wider front, but one where his vulnerable left flank was protected by a sheer wall of rock towering nearly 1,000m over the Middle Gate. There was another advantage to be gained from the site he chose. At the Middle Gate the Phokians at some time in the past had built a defensive wall designed to protect them from their arch-enemies to the north, the Thessalians.

THE DAYS BEFORE THE BATTLE

The old Phokian wall was in a ruinous condition, so the Greeks immediately set about repairing it. But the strength of the Thermopylae position was lessened by the existence of a number of flanking routes either southwards or eastwards round the gates. At the most dangerous of these, the Anopaia path, Leonidas stationed 1,000 Phokian hoplites, local men, who might be supposed to be the best watch-and-ward force in a situation where such knowledge would be at a premium. They also had immediately the most to lose. Herodotos specifically says (7.175.2) that the Greeks knew nothing of this mountain track until they learned of it from the people of Trachis on the spot, a salutary reminder to us

OPPOSITE **A general view of Thermopylae, looking south-east from above Lamia. The famous pass can be seen in the far distance below Kallidromos and by the Malian Gulf. Today the silt brought down by the River Spercheios has advanced the coastline by some 5km, though the plain is still marshy. (Author's collection)**

▲ 701   Height in metres

━━━━   Anopaia path as described by Herodotos (7.215–217.1)

Modern check-points after Wallace (1980)
A.   Eleftherokhori
B.   Palaiodhrakospilia
C.   Dhrakospilia

Sperchelos

Ancient road

Ancient coastline

Present coastline

Malian Gulf
(now salt flats)

Ancient coastline

Melas

Persian Camp
ʌ ʌ ʌ ʌ ʌ

West Gate

Middle Gate

Phokian Wall

East Gate

● Alpenoi

Xerias

● Trachis
▲ 701

Asopos

🏛 Anthela

● Hot springs

Hillock of Kolonos

Black-Buttocks' Stone

Mount Oita

Asopos Gorge

━ Route of the Immortals

Eleftherokhori
Ⓐ

Anopaia (upland plain of Nevropolis)

Ⓑ
Palaiodhrakospilia

▲ 950

▲ 1042

Dhrakospilia

Ⓒ   ▲ 1162

N
↑

K a l l i d r o m o s

Anopaia path

▲ 1302

▲ 1399

▲ 950

| 0 | 2 miles |
| 0 | 2km |

An aerial shot of Thermopylae, looking south-west towards the northern flank of Kallidromos. The defile is less than 6.5km long and, at the time of the battle, ran between precipitous mountains and the sea (the hatched area in the bottom right). It was extremely narrow at both ends, but widened in the middle, where hot springs lay. (Author's collection)

Thermopylae is so called because of the hot sulphurous springs that still rise there today. The carbonic acid and lime in these thermal springs, just to the right here, gives the landscape the appearance of crusty grey rock. In the distance, towards the east, is the site of the Greek position. (Author's collection)

that such events did not involve people equipped with trained staffs and good maps, but people who had never faced a war on this scale before or fought at such distances from their homes.

After the Persian host had arrived at Thermopylae, there was a delay of four days before the actual assault began. In that well-known story of Herodotos (7.208.2–3) the Spartans, calmly awaiting the Persian onslaught, passed their time in taking exercise and combing their hair in front of the Phokian wall. Questioned about this, so Herodotos' tale continues (7.209.3), the Persian-allied exiled Spartan king Demaratos is said to have told Xerxes that combing their hair was a sign that the Spartans were preparing for battle. If this was so, then an indispensable piece of equipment for any self-respecting Spartiate was his comb. On early fifth-century warrior figurines from Sparta, the hair is normally dressed in four locks falling to the front, two on each shoulder, and four to the back. The beard is short and pointed and the upper lip is normally shaven. Apparently, every year upon entering office the ephors would order the Spartans to 'cut their moustaches and obey the law' (Aristotle *ap.* Plutarch *Kleomenes* 9.3).

The point of Herodotos' story is that the Spartans, at some point in their history, adopted the idea of wearing the hair long as a symbolic reminder of belligerent arrogance, almost inverted snobbery. This is certainly the view promoted by Xenophon (*Lakedaimonion politeia* 11.3) when he explains how men who had just entered manhood were not only permitted to don the highly prized crimson military cloak, but also to wear their hair long in the belief that it made them look taller, more dignified and more terrifying. Hardly surprising, therefore, to find young Spartan men entering battle with their hair immaculately groomed and oiled, 'looking cheerful and impressive' (Xenophon *Lakedaimonion politeia* 13.9).

Whether or not Herodotos' story is apocryphal, it does illustrate the awe in which the Spartans were held, not by the Persians, but by their fellow Greeks. In his version of events Diodoros says (11.5.4–5) that Xerxes sent envoys to order the Greeks to surrender their arms and depart to their own territories, promising to grant them more and better lands if they did so. This is not too improbable, since diplomacy was part-and-parcel of the Persian art of war, but in Diodoros' account Xerxes' demand elicits a most un-laconic reply from Leonidas. Far better is Plutarch's version of the reply: '*molōn labe*' – 'come and get them' (*Moralia* 225D).

THE FIRST DAY

Herodotos' explanation for the four-day lull is that Xerxes was waiting 'in constant expectation that the Greeks would make good their escape' (7.210.1). What was a diminutive stone wall to a monarch who had marched his army across the Hellespont and sailed his navy through the land behind Mount Athos? A quick scuffle in the hot dust of Thermopylae should see Leonidas and his rag-tag band off, and the pass safely in Xerxes' hands. So, early in the morning of his fifth day before Thermopylae, Xerxes gave the order for a frontal assault on the Greeks obstinately lodged in the pass. The Median and Kissian contingents marched forwards to carry out their king's wishes. Herodotos is somewhat vague about the epic fight that ensued, but he does make the obvious point that the Persians could not make full use of their numerical superiority because of the confined terrain, and also remarks that they were 'using shorter spears than the Greeks' (7.211.2). The Persians, who were principally armed with bows, clearly committed themselves to an engagement that could only suit the enemy.

Surprise is a weapon. Often underestimated, it is one of the most effective and cheapest of all force multipliers as well as one of the most versatile. It is possible to surprise your foe not only in time or place of battle but in the manner of fighting. The Spartans, representing the only force in Greece approaching what we moderns would call a professional army, brought the tactical development of the hoplite phalanx to its highest degree. Turning and retreating in what seemed a disorderly

A PERSIAN SCOUT RECONNOITRES THE GREEK POSITION
(pages 66–67)

All professional armies form, to some extent, closed communities with their own customs and standards of behaviour. This was no less so with the Spartan army. Yet in the ancient Greek world Sparta, with its intimate relationship between social organization and military power, was the exception in this regard. Sparta was a totally militarized society, and the transformation began before puberty, when a Spartan boy was fully immersed in a disciplined environment in which only the pre-state warrior ethic was allowed to penetrate. No other Greek state appears to have put its young males through such a rigorous regime as the Spartan *agōgē*, and by and large, there was a prejudice, born from the militia ethos of the citizen-farmer, against training in war.

Though war was (and still is) not a normal human condition, the Spartan aggressive and warlike fighting spirit was a vital yet intangible quality whose roots lay in male bonding, which was fostered and preserved though a definite group identity. It was this complex chemistry that allowed the Spartiate unflinchingly to face death, battle after battle. But the personal bravery of a single individual does not decide the issue on the actual day of battle, rather the bravery of the unit as a whole, and the latter rests on the good opinion and confidence that each individual places in the unit of which he is a member. It is for this reason that the Spartans fully recognized the vital importance of regular exercise to maintain unit excellence, and even on active service soldiers were expected to keep their minds and bodies – especially the legs, arms and neck – fit through gymnastics and games (Xenophon, *Lakedaimonion politeia* 5.9, 12.5).

This was certainly the case when a Persian mounted scout (1) approached the Greek position at Thermopylae. On that day it was the Spartans (2) who happened to be stationed in sight, outside the reconstructed Phokian wall (3). With their arms piled near to hand, some of the soldiers were stripped and oiled for exercise, while others were combing their exceptionally long hair, a sign that they were preparing to risk their lives; and all paying him not the slightest attention. The scout may have been utterly astonished, but to the busy soldiers this was just the Spartan way of doing things. Meanwhile, two clothed guards kept watch on the wall (4).

Physical exercises noted for their all-round benefits, as opposed to those that are violent or specialized, were probably popular with soldiers on campaign, so some of the Spartans in this scene are ball-playing (5). This particular ball game, known as *episkyros* or common-ball, was played between opposing teams of equal number. A centre line was scratched in the dust between the two teams and a goal line behind each. The ball was set on the middle line and the team that got it first threw it over the opposition, whose task was to grab the ball while it was in motion and throw it back the other way. The game continued until one team had pushed the other over its goal line. The ball itself was small and hard, covered in leather and stuffed with horsehair.

It is said that Herakles, his skin fused horribly to a poisoned cloak, plunged headlong into the nearest stream. But these waters increased the poison's burning power, and they have run scalding-hot forever after and are called Thermopylae. The waters (43°C) are said to be good for the cure of sciatica. (Author's collection)

The Middle Gate seen from the mound of the last stand, looking west towards the Persian position and the thermal springs – the white building is a popular spa and restaurant. To the left Kallidromos towers over Thermopylae, while the ancient coastline would have been just to the right of the National Highway. (Author's collection)

fashion and then, once they had tricked the Persians into pursuing them, changing direction in an instantaneous about-turn and 'inflict[ing] in the new struggle innumerable casualties' (Herodotos 7.211.3). Clearly such tactics, which denied the Persians a static target for their customary hail of arrows, had the effect of bringing about a series of hand-to-hand encounters in which the Spartans had the upper hand.

It was growing late in the afternoon, probably about the same time that the Greek fleet was achieving its tactical (if limited) success against the Persians, when Xerxes decided to clear the pass ahead before sundown. The crack troops of the empire, the Immortals themselves,

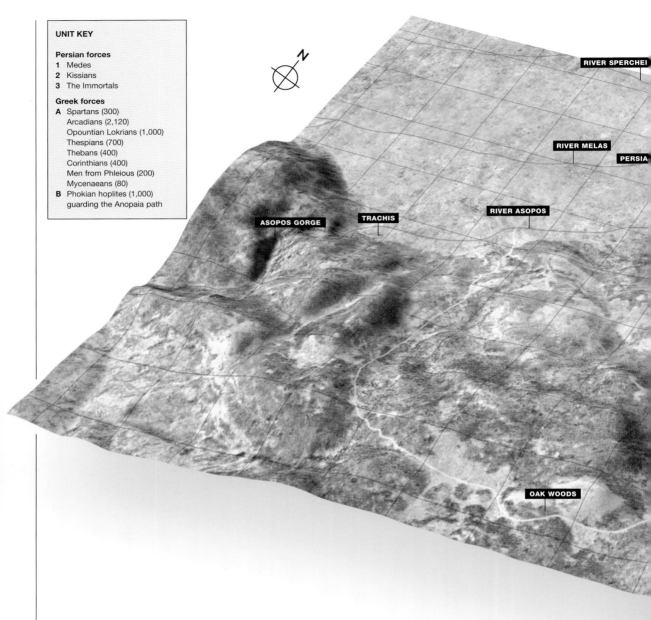

UNIT KEY

Persian forces
1 Medes
2 Kissians
3 The Immortals

Greek forces
A Spartans (300)
   Arcadians (2,120)
   Opountian Lokrians (1,000)
   Thespians (700)
   Thebans (400)
   Corinthians (400)
   Men from Phleious (200)
   Mycenaeans (80)
B Phokian hoplites (1,000)
   guarding the Anopaia path

RIVER SPERCHEI

RIVER MELAS

PERSIA

RIVER ASOPOS

ASOPOS GORGE

TRACHIS

OAK WOODS

▼ EVENTS

1. **Following their arrival at Thermopylae, the Persians have established their main camp near the so-called West Gate, the western entrance to the Thermopylae pass. However, they wait four days before beginning their assault. In the meantime, the Persians send envoys to the Greeks ordering them to surrender, but the Greeks stand firm.**

2. **In the centre of the pass, known as the Middle Gate, the Greeks have repaired the Phokian wall and taken up their main position behind it.**

3. **So that there can be no surprise from that quarter, Leonidas has detailed the 1,000 Phokians to guard the Anopaia path, the mountain track over the Kallidromos range to the south of the main positions.**

4. **On the morning of the fifth day following the Persians' arrival, Xerxes orders a frontal assault on the Middle Gate by the Medes and Kissians. Despite their superior numbers, the Medes and Kissians fail to break through.**

5. **The Greek tactics include feigning disorderly retreat and tricking the Persians into pursuing them, before turning on them and inflicting casualties. Such manoeuvering also mitigates the threat posed by hails of Persian arrow fire.**

6. **Late in the afternoon of the same day, the crack troops of Xerxes' empire, the Immortals, are launched at the Greeks – but they, too, fail to achieve a breakthrough at the Middle Gate.**

THE FIRST DAY AT THERMOPYLAE

The Persian frontal assault on the Middle Gate is repulsed by the Greeks

Note: gridlines are shown at intervals of 1km/1,094 yards

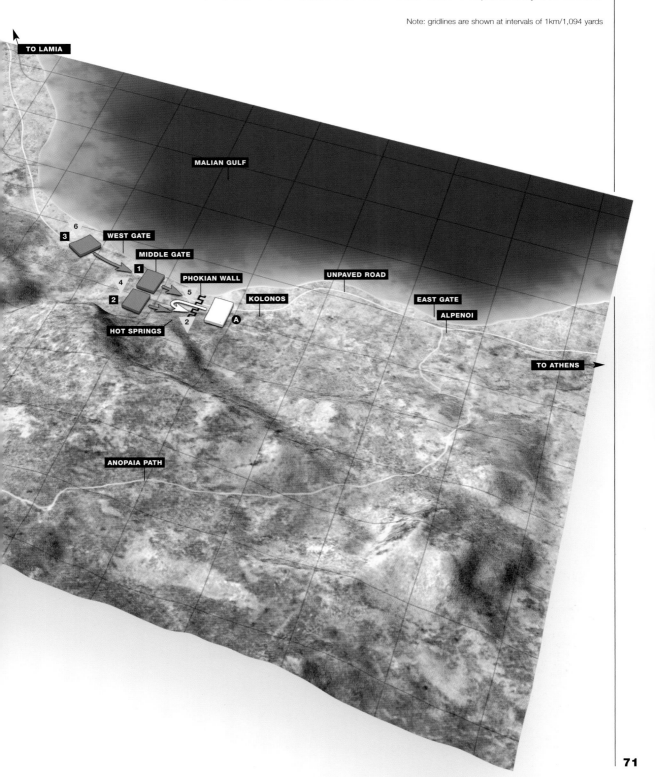

TO LAMIA

MALIAN GULF

6
3
WEST GATE

MIDDLE GATE

1
PHOKIAN WALL
4
5
UNPAVED ROAD
2
KOLONOS
EAST GATE
2
A
ALPENOI
HOT SPRINGS

TO ATHENS

ANOPAIA PATH

On the southern flank of the Middle Gate the heights of Kallidromos towers stark and sheer, a defensive wall nearly 1,000m high upon which Leonidas anchored his left flank. Here, looking from the site of the Thermopylae monument, they are seen towering above the mound of the last stand. (Author's collection)

were ordered up and 'advanced to the attack in full confidence of bringing the business to a quick and easy end' (Herodotos 7.211.1). But they were no more successful than the Medes and Kissians had been before them.

THE SECOND DAY

The second day's fighting was much like the first, with no better success for the Persians, despite the Greeks being so few in number. Herodotos does add, however, that the latter fought in relays, with each contingent, apart from the Phokians, taking 'its turn in the line' (7.212.2). Thus those not engaged had the opportunity to lick their wounds and catch their breath. At the end of the day, albeit a few Greeks having been killed, Xerxes was no nearer to his objective, and we can well imagine his increasing frustration and irritation at the turn of events. Yet to Xerxes the only immediate route lay through the pass ahead.

What the Persian high command lacked, although they had well-informed Greek advisers in tow, was that salient thing, local knowledge. Since there were no maps, local knowledge was of prime consequence in ancient warfare: something that meant that the invader of a foreign land was always at a grave disadvantage. Still, traitors and deserters are the common currency of war, and so it was for the Persians when a local man from Trachis, Ephialtes, son of Eurydemos, came forwards in the hope of receiving a worthwhile reward from Xerxes. He offered to show the Persians the hard-to-follow mountain track and guide them along it and back down to the East Gate to take the Greek position in the rear.

Starting at the West Gate, this route followed the valley of the Asopos, passing through a precipitous gorge. The route climbed up the hillside about a kilometre east of the gorge, the easiest and shortest ascent up the mountainside, and then ran over the hills above the gorge and stretched along the spine of the Kallidromos range, ending at Alpēnoi, the first settlement of Lokris. Leonidas was of course aware of this route and

Possible remains of the Phokian wall. Excavated by Spiros Marinatos just prior to World War II, the wall started with a tower and then zigzagged downhill. It probably continued across level ground to terminate at another tower. There was a narrow gateway next to the upper tower. (Author's collection)

NIGHT MARCH OF THE IMMORTALS (pages 74–75)

'At about the time the lamps were lit', in the evocative words of Herodotos (7.215.1), Hydarnes (1) and the Immortals moved out from their camp, guided by the local shepherd, Ephialtes (2), to take the mountain track of which he had informed Xerxes. All night the Immortals toiled up the winding path until, as the sky began to grey in the east, the ground levelled off and they entered a small upland plain. Here they lengthened their steps and moved smartly along under oak trees. Last year's leaves lay thick on the ground and, as Herodotos continues, 'the marching feet made a loud swishing and rustling in the fallen leaves' (7.218.1). Ahead of them the silence of the windless night was broken as the Phokian hoplites (3) hastily donned their battle garb.

By this date many hoplites had abandoned the bronze bell-shaped corselet (*thōrax*) commonly worn by their grandfathers and instead wore the lighter, more flexible linen corselet (*linothōrax*, 4). It was made up of numerous layers of linen glued together to form a stiff shirt, which could be reinforced with plates or scales made of iron or bronze. The body piece of this shirt had armholes cut out and below the waist it was cut, for ease of movement, into

two overlapping layers of strips (*pteruges*). This wrapped around the torso and was laced together on the left-hand side, where the join was protected by the large hoplite shield (*aspis*, 5). A U-shaped yoke (6), which bent forwards over the shoulders and was tied to the chest, completed the corselet.

The Immortals are shown dressed and equipped for war, in a manner very different to the palace costume shown on the Sousa brick panels and Persepolis limestone reliefs. Each wears a loose-fitting tunic, brightly coloured and richly embroidered, close-fitting trousers, equally as colourful, and the traditional cloth *tiara* (7). Around the neck is worn a torque of twisted gold, a mark of the Great King's favour. Their weapons are the composite bow (8), which was carried in a combined bow-case and quiver-holder (*gorytos*, 9), and a short iron-headed spear (10) with a silver, spherical counterweight. The *gorytos* hangs from a waist belt on the left side, a position that allows for a rapid rate of fire, while on the right the traditional long, straight double-edged dagger (*akinakes*, 11) is worn as a handy sidearm. For defence a lightweight figure-of-eight-shaped wicker shield (*gerrhon*, 12), made of canes threaded through rawhide, is carried.

had stationed the local Phokian contingent, 1,000 strong, to guard it. Herodotos (7.215.1) clearly implies that all the Immortals – that is, 10,000 men – accompanied Ephialtes, and there is no real reason to dispute him here as the route he guided them along was comparatively easy.

THE THIRD DAY

Kallidromos (meaning 'beautiful running track') is the name used by Strabo (9.428) and not Herodotos. Along its crest there are two parallel ridges, between which lies a narrow but fertile upland plain that was, at the time, fringed by dense oak woods. 'This, then,' says Herodotos, 'was the mountain track, which the Persians took, after crossing the Asopos' (7.217.1). Just as dawn was breaking, Hydarnes and the Immortals reached the Phokian position. Both sides were surprised, but the Immortals rapidly drew their bows and opened fire on the Phokians. After a lofted volley or two, the citizen-militia, believing themselves to be the primary target, retired to a high position and prepared to sell their lives as dearly as they could. The disciplined professionals paid no heed to them, however, but continued on their way to take the main Greek force in the rear.

The first warning to the Greeks of 'the death that was coming with the dawn' (Herodotos 7.219.1) came from the seer (*mantis*), Megistias of Akarnania, when he examined the sacrificial victims. Leonidas first received the news that the Persians were crossing the mountains from deserters, who came in during the night, and then from lookouts posted on the heights who ran down to inform him just after dawn. So began the famous last day at Thermopylae.

One of the many tracks that criss-cross Kallidromos, and possible candidate for the Anopaia path as it ascends towards the Nevropolis plain. At the time of Thermopylae this mountainside was covered in oak woods, but even today, after deforestation, it is still easy to lose your way without the services of a local guide. (Author's collection)

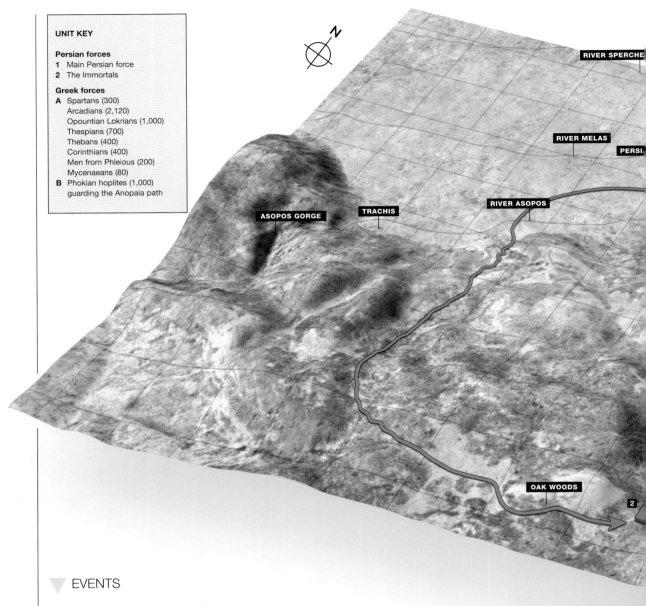

UNIT KEY

Persian forces
1 Main Persian force
2 The Immortals

Greek forces
A Spartans (300)
   Arcadians (2,120)
   Opountian Lokrians (1,000)
   Thespians (700)
   Thebans (400)
   Corinthians (400)
   Men from Phleious (200)
   Mycenaeans (80)
B Phokian hoplites (1,000)
   guarding the Anopaia path

RIVER SPERCHE

RIVER MELAS

PERSI

TRACHIS

ASOPOS GORGE

RIVER ASOPOS

OAK WOODS

2

▼ EVENTS

1. **On the morning of the second day, Xerxes orders a further assault on the Greek position, throwing fresh troops into battle. The attacks fare no better than those on the first day, though. The various Greek contingents take it in turns to fight in the front line.**

2. **Ephialtes, a local man from Trachis betrays the Greek cause and reveals the existence of an upper path to the Persians. The Anopaia path is a hard to follow mountain track leading to the village of Alpenoi. At nightfall on the second day, the Immortals, led by the Persian noble Hydarnes, set off on their mission to turn the Greek position.**

3. **At dawn, the Hydarnes and the Immortals reach the Phokian hoplites guarding the Anopaia path; both sides are surprised. The Persians open up with volleys of arrow fire, and the Phokians retreat to higher ground, awaiting the Persian attack. However, the destruction of the Phokians is not the primary objective of the Persians.**

4. **The Immortals pay no more attention to the Phokians, but hurry on to reach the East Gate and thereby take the main Greek position in the rear.**

5. **Early in the morning of the third day, news reaches Leonidas of the imminent arrival of the Persian flanking force. Leonidas holds a council of war, and it is decided that, before their escape route is cut, most of the Greeks should leave Thermopylae. The only Greeks remaining are the 300 Spartans, 700 Thespians, and 400 Thebans.**

THE SECOND DAY AT THERMOPYLAE
The Persians outflank the main Greek positions via the Anopaia path

Note: gridlines are shown at intervals of 1km/1,094 yards

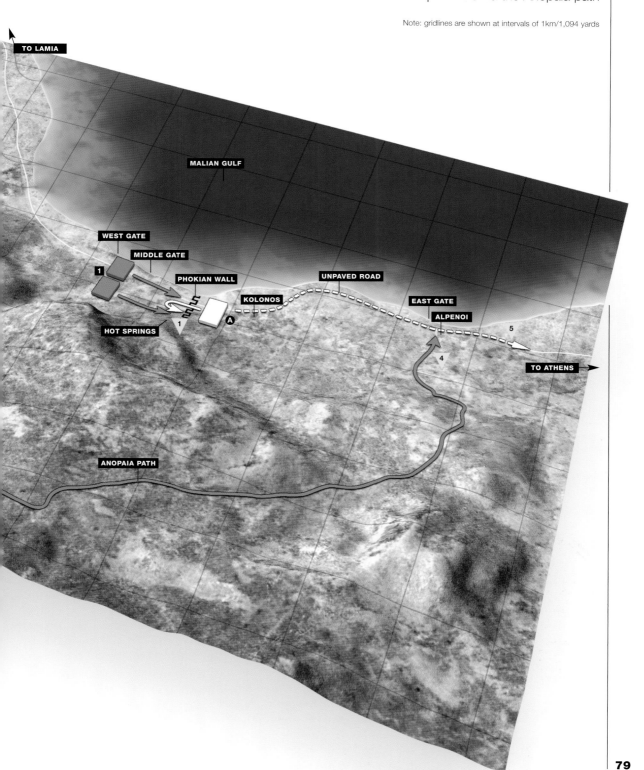

TO LAMIA

MALIAN GULF

WEST GATE

MIDDLE GATE

1

PHOKIAN WALL

UNPAVED ROAD

KOLONOS

EAST GATE

HOT SPRINGS

1

A

ALPENOI

5

4

TO ATHENS

ANOPAIA PATH

It was before dawn, on the final day of the battle, that the seer, Megistias of Akarnania, was able to foretell the coming doom of Leonidas and his men. This detail of the left-hand frieze of the Thermopylae monument shows Megistias looking skywards. He was said to be a descendant of Melampos, who understood the language of birds. (Author's collection)

Upon receipt of the news that their position was about to be turned, Leonidas held a council of war, which revealed a split in the allies' opinions between retreat and resistance. Leonidas ordered the allies to retreat, with the exception of 700 Thespians and 400 Thebans, because, in Herodotos' own opinion, he perceived there was a lack of will to fight, and did not want such a potentially damaging and divisive split to be made public. His decision to stay with his 300 Spartans, Herodotos continues, was motivated by a Delphic oracle, which prophesied that either Sparta 'must be laid waste by the foreigner or a Spartan king be killed' (7.220.2). However true this may be, and the oracle could be a *post eventum* attempt to boost morale after the death of the Spartan king, there was a much more prosaic reason for Leonidas staying and engaging the Persians on the third day: the need to buy time for the other Greeks to escape. If the whole Greek force had retreated, the Persians, with their strength in cavalry and lightly armed troops, would have soon overtaken them and destroyed them. Hence a fighting rearguard would be necessary.

The inclusion of Leonidas and his Spartans, presumably with their attendant helots, was inevitable, since he could hardly hope to be obeyed if he ordered others to stay put, while he and the Spartans departed. He may have called for volunteers. So, as Herodotos says, all the allies went off in obedience to Leonidas' orders, except the Thespians and Thebans, the latter under compulsion because Leonidas wanted to keep them as hostages, the former simply because they 'refused to desert Leonidas and his men' (7.222). As for the Thebans, as was pointed out long ago by an indignant Plutarch (*Moralia* 865D), if Leonidas had really wanted to keep them hostage, he would have sent them off under guard with the rest of the Greeks. Besides, retaining people of doubtful loyalty in such a situation would have surely weakened Leonidas' position.

And why should we not believe that the Thespians, and for that matter the Thebans too, volunteered to stay with Leonidas? Some indication that men were willing to volunteer is shown by the case of Megistias. When Leonidas tried to dismiss the seer, a man not expected to stand in the front line and fight, he refused to go, sending his only son instead, who was serving with the army as a hoplite. Simonides, in an epitaph he personally put up for friendship's sake, said of Megistias that 'he scorned to save himself, but shared the Spartans' grave' (Herodotos 7.228.3).

On the morning of what would be his last day, Leonidas, in the words of Plutarch, 'passed the word to his soldiers to eat breakfast in the expectation that they would be dining in Hades' (*Moralia* 225D). Laconic gallows humour, maybe so, but this was an oblique reference to the fact that living Spartans when in Sparta took just one compulsory meal a day, the communal evening mess meal. In the pale light of the early morning, the Spartans at Thermopylae, no doubt, also found time to comb their hair and prepare fresh garlands.

The hillock of Kolonos has been identified as the site of the last stand. The sandy mound was excavated by Marinatos and hundreds of Persian arrowheads were discovered. Even at the very end, rather than close in for the kill, the Persians relied on aerial bombardment to finish the decimated Greeks. (Author's collection)

The Great King celebrated the rising of the sun by pouring libations, and then waited until 'about the time that the market-place is full' (Herodotos 7.223.1) before giving the order for his army to move forwards. This evocative Herodotean phrase places the time of day somewhere between nine and ten in the morning, before all sensible Mediterranean people retire into the shade like lizards to escape the 'teeth of the sun'. Herodotos adds that Xerxes had been asked to do so by Ephialtes, presumably so that Xerxes' attack on the Middle Gate was intended to coincide with Hydarnes' blocking of the East Gate. In the event it appears that Hydarnes was late, but this is understandable in view of the difficulty of synchronizing a military operation of this nature.

The Persians were met by the Greeks, who on the two previous days had occupied the narrowest part of the pass by the Phokian wall, and relieved the front-line troops in relays. But today Leonidas changed his tactics and led them into the wider part of the pass so that all were to be committed at once. As we already know, the noteworthy feature of a Spartan battle line, and on this particular occasion we should also include the gallant Thespians and Thebans, was that it advanced in an organized and measured way to the music of the *aulos*. The Spartans had enough confidence and skill to do without the initial advantage, which most Greek armies sought from the impact of as fast a charge as a hoplite could achieve with the burden of his arms and armour under the Mediterranean sun.

Meanwhile the Persians were beginning to flex their bows and eye the unbroken shield wall of slow moving hoplites. It was at this point that the Greeks made their customary blood sacrifice and continued the advance. Then, as the enemy's missiles began to

The wounded and the dying, as depicted on the right-hand frieze of the modern monument at Thermopylae. There is a human dimension to warfare that is too easily overlooked. Here is a poignant reminder of the human reality of the battlefield on which so many Greek and Persian soldiers fought, suffered, and died. (Author's collection)

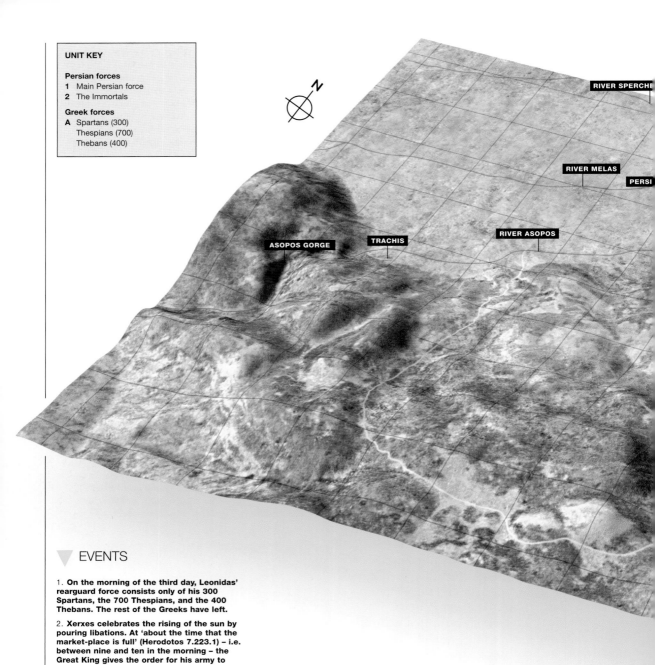

UNIT KEY

Persian forces
1 Main Persian force
2 The Immortals

Greek forces
A Spartans (300)
   Thespians (700)
   Thebans (400)

RIVER SPERCH

RIVER MELAS

PERSI

RIVER ASOPOS

ASOPOS GORGE

TRACHIS

▼ EVENTS

1. **On the morning of the third day, Leonidas' rearguard force consists only of his 300 Spartans, the 700 Thespians, and the 400 Thebans. The rest of the Greeks have left.**

2. **Xerxes celebrates the rising of the sun by pouring libations. At 'about the time that the market-place is full' (Herodotos 7.223.1) – i.e. between nine and ten in the morning – the Great King gives the order for his army to attack the Middle Gate once more. He has calculated that Hydarnes will be descending Kallidromos at this time, and the attack is designed to coincide with this.**

3. **Leonidas advances his miniscule force out of the narrowest part of the Middle Gate into a wider part of the pass, so that all his troops can be committed at once.**

4. **The Greeks clash with the advancing Persians. During the furious battle, Leonidas is killed. The Greeks eventually win a violent and prolonged struggle for his body.**

5. **Meanwhile, after their all-night march along the Anopaia path, Hydarnes and the Immortals have arrived at the Greek rear, thereby blocking their escape through the East Gate. The trap is now closed for Leonidas and his rearguard force.**

6. **The Greeks withdraw back into the narrow part of the pass, crossing the Phokian wall and taking up a position beyond on the hillock of Kolonos, where Herodotos says 'the stone lion in memory of Leonidas stands today' (7.225.2). The Thebans break away from the rest of the Greeks, and run towards the enemy, throwing down their weapons. They are either killed or taken prisoner.**

7. **The Persian main force breaks through the Phokian wall defences, and Hydarnes and the Immortals advance towards the Greek rear. Leonidas and his men die fighting to the last on the hillock, overwhelmed by Persian arrow fire. Xerxes orders the Spartan king to be identified, and his head cut off and placed on a pole for all to see.**

THE THIRD DAY AT THERMOPYLAE
The remaining Greeks are finally overwhelmed on the hillock of Kolonos

Note: gridlines are shown at intervals of 1km/1,094 yards

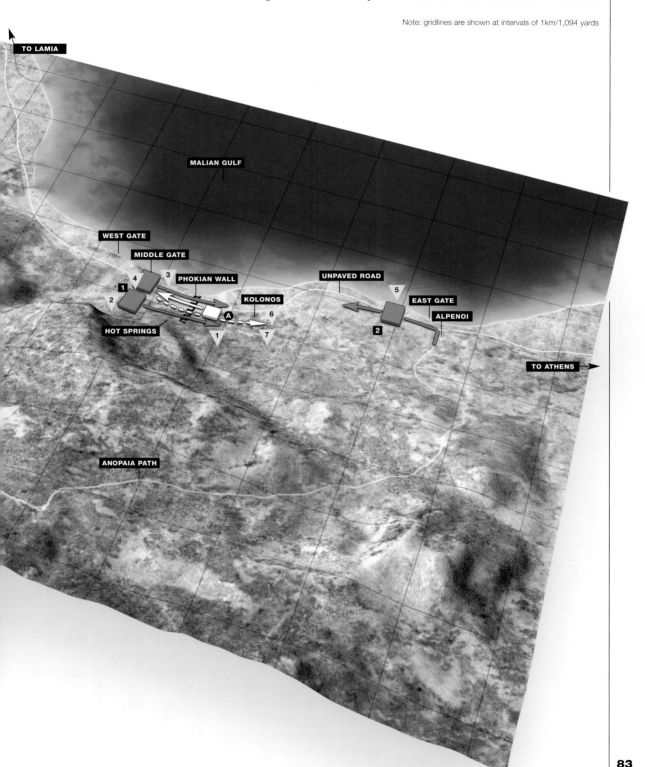

TO LAMIA

MALIAN GULF

WEST GATE

MIDDLE GATE

PHOKIAN WALL

UNPAVED ROAD

KOLONOS

EAST GATE

ALPENOI

HOT SPRINGS

TO ATHENS

ANOPAIA PATH

The death of Leonidas, a detail of the left-hand frieze of the Thermopylae monument. After a struggle somewhat reminiscent of Homer, the Spartans gain control over the dead body of their king. His death was subsequently supported by an oracle and interpreted as the necessary sacrifice that allowed the Greeks to defeat the Persians in the war. (Author's collection)

fly, Leonidas probably broke with Spartan custom and ordered his men to sprint towards the Persians, whereupon a furious engagement commenced. The king, leading from the front of the mêlée, had no mechanical means of communicating; his primary function that desperate morning was to maintain the morale of his small command at the highest possible pitch by personal example. Herodotos claims the losses among the Persians were even heavier than those sustained on the previous two days, many of the enemy being forced into the sea or trampled underfoot by their comrades 'as their commanders plied their whips indiscriminately' (7.223.3). Even allowing for a degree of exaggeration, he may well be right. Once again the Greeks were denying the Persian archers a static target at which to shoot, by advancing (or running) into contact, and if they were deployed on a broader front the losses they would have inflicted would have been all the greater.

Here they fought with reckless abandon. But then Leonidas himself fell, and not only would this have left the Greeks momentarily leaderless, but the Spartans would never have been prepared to leave the king's body where it lay, in the dust and debris of battle. Thus, far from the Greeks retreating, an even more furious struggle developed over the king's dead body. In a scene that might have come straight out of the *Iliad*, Herodotos describes how there was 'much shoving' (*ōthismos … pollōs*, 7.225.1), and, after flinging the enemy back four times, the Greeks dragged the body back within their battle-worn ranks.

At last, however, the remaining Greeks learned of the approaching Immortals and withdrew back into the narrow part of the pass crossing the Phokian wall and taking up a position on the hillock, where Herodotos says 'the stone lion in memory of Leonidas stands today' (7.225.2). Here the Greeks took their stand, except for the Thebans, who broke away from the rest and ran towards the enemy, throwing aside what weapons they had and holding out their hands in a token of surrender. Some of them were inevitably killed by men who were still hot for blood, but the majority of those who gave themselves up were taken prisoner. They were branded with the Great King's mark.

The final act in the drama was soon over. Herodotos tells of the last stand that none of the defenders had spears left, and were fighting 'with their swords, if they had them, and, if not, with their hands and teeth' (7.225.3). But the attackers pushed down the Phokian wall and poured through the breach, and Hydarnes and his men arrived at last to take them in the rear. Significantly Herodotos says that the Persians 'finally overwhelmed them with missile weapons' (7.225.3), so even at the finish the Persian weapon of choice was the arrow, safely released at a distance.

BETWEEN HISTORY AND LEGEND

Splendid it maybe, but we cannot press Herodotos' dramatic account of the last stand too closely, since we are bound to ask how he learned the details if all the Greeks were killed. Of course it is possible that some of the Thebans who survived were still near enough to see what happened. Intriguingly, Herodotos says of the Thebans that as they were surrendering they were shouting to the Persians they had 'come to Thermopylae against their will' (7.233.1). There is no reason to doubt that at least some of the Thebans, having decided that they had done enough in the aid of a cause that was clearly hopeless, opted to surrender and survive rather than to face a certain death.

Yet there is a strong element of bias – probably derived from an Athenian source – in Herodotos' remarks about the Thebans both here and elsewhere in his account of the battle. For instance, he says (2.205.3) that Leonidas was particularly anxious to pick up the contingent from Thebes he took with him to Thermopylae, because of serious accusations of medisim against the Thebans. In reality it is possible that the Spartans were still confident that the Thebans would support them, though they presumably hoped for more than the 400 hoplites they got, given that Thebes was the principal *polis* of Boiotia. Perhaps these Thebans with Leonidas represented those in Thebes who were inclined to resist the Persians. As Diodoros indeed says, they were 'of the other party' (11.4.7). Later, after Thermopylae, all the Boiotians except Thespiai (an enemy of Thebes) and Plataia (an ally of Athens) medized, so that the reputation of all the Thebans was especially blackened when the Persians were eventually beaten back in the following year. Posterity would immortalize the Three Hundred and they alone.

The Thermopylae legend, the legend of a glorious defeat, was not slow to be born. Herodotos (7.224.1) was proud to relate that he had learned the names of the Three Hundred. As expected, therefore, he only mentions the helot attendants of these heroic Spartans to say one of them pointed his blind master in the direction of battle, and then shamefully 'took to his heels' (7.229.1). Yet in the aftermath of battle passing reference is made to helot corpses lying on the battlefield (8.25.1), from which it seems fair to suggest that many of the 300 helots had fought alongside the Spartan hoplites as lightly armed troops. This was certainly the case with the helots at Plataia the following year, for Herodotos says they were in some fashion 'armed for war' (9.28). It seems that helots provided their Spartan masters with more than the economic basis of their unique lifestyle, as they also accompanied them on campaign where they not only carried equipment and provisions, but pitched tents, fetched water, cooked, and, armed with javelins or alternatively slings, even fought. Helots ranked for ancient theorists, too, as people 'between slave and free'.

The impact of Thermopylae was mainly ideological, a fight between free men and slaves, and so was born the leitmotif that the Greeks in general, and the Spartans in particular, fought of their own free will but in obedience to their laws or customs (Herodotos 7.104.3). As spearmen they sought open battle, which they fought hand to hand. The Persians, on the other hand, were subject to the whims of a single man and only fought coerced by the whip (Herodotos 7.103.4, 223.3). They were servile cowards, because as bowmen they sought to avoid close-quarter combat. In Persia the Great King was the state, while in Greece the hoplites formed the state. Separating myth from reality is difficult, particularly in the case of this legendary battle.

So, whilst posterity remembers the Three Hundred who gave their lives willingly at Thermopylae, few will recall that over twice that number of Thespians died on the same day. The contingent of 700 Thespians, with their *stratēgos* who bore the Dionysiac name of Dithyrambos, probably comprised all the adult males of Thespiai who qualified for

A statue group (Athens, National Archaeological Museum, 3335) of Aphrodite, Eros and Pan, from Delos (c. 100 BC). Wanton Eros, who is only intermittently under his mother's control, is not a deity normally associated with the hard-bitten Spartans. However, just prior to battle they 'sacrificed to the god of love'. (Author's collection)

THE FALL OF LEONIDAS (pp 86–87)

On the famous last day at Thermopylae the remaining Greeks did not wait passively for the assault. Instead, according to Herodotos (7.223.2), they moved out farther into the broader part of the pass than they had previously done. The fighting was furious, for when most of their ash-wood spears, the main weapon of the hoplite, were broken they began to use their swords. Worse still, it was then that Leonidas (1) fell, and this would not only have left the Greeks temporarily leaderless, but probably have made the surviving Spartans refuse even to contemplate retreat until they had recovered their king's body. Herodotos says there was 'much shoving' (7.225.1), until the Greeks recovered it, flinging the enemy back four times. The fall of the king was the catalyst for an even more ferocious display of valour on the part of the Spartans, conspicuous in their crimson tunics (2). Among the many Persians who fell fighting over such a valuable trophy were two half-brothers of Xerxes.

The Spartans, blinded by the dust kicked up by thousands of feet on all sides, fought furiously in what seemed a sea of Persians, who fought with *sagaris* (3), *akinakes* (4), spear and bow. For an exhausting hour or so, the throat-parched troops continued to claw away at each other.

The lawgiver Lykourgos, it is said by Xenophon, had ordered the Spartans to wear crimson cloaks and tunics, since these garments were 'least effeminate and most warlike', and to carry bronze-faced shields, since bronze was 'quickest to polish and slow to tarnish' (*Lakedaimonion politeia* 11.3). The Spartan military cloak, known as a *tribōn* or 'worn cloak', is often described as being 'mean' (*phaulos*), that is, thin as opposed to short. Indeed, austerity was the keynote to the Spartan lifestyle, and a Spartiate would visually emphasize his toughness by making use of a single cloak, summer and winter, allowed to wear thin and never washed. This particular article of his uniform was treasured above all else, so much so, if we are to believe Plutarch (*Lykourgos* 27.1), he would be buried without grave goods, but wrapped in his crimson cloak and crowned with an olive wreath. Of course, for purely practical reasons, the cloak was discarded before battle commenced and left behind in camp. Even so, as Plutarch (*Moralia* 238F) observes, the crimson-coloured tunic alone would have aroused terror in the inexperienced opponent and helped to disguise battle wounds. The tunic (*chitȳn*) itself could be a relatively thick woollen garment, though at this time it was generally becoming lighter and sometimes linen replaced wool. It was usually sleeveless, and extended from shoulder to mid thigh.

While uniform, in the sense of a national military costume principally fashioned from cloth and codified according to regulations, is a comparatively modern concept, for Sparta, with its intimate relationship between social organization and military power, the adoption of distinctive dress went beyond the mere idea of looking different from one's foes. For the strength of Sparta's army lay not only in its professionalism but also in its formidable appearance; this was intentionally designed to strike terror into the hearts of Sparta's enemies.

hoplite service. It was an extraordinary muster that emptied the *polis* of its property-holding citizenry. Various explanations have been offered for their remarkable courage, ranging from the fatalistic notion that nothing remained for them in a medizing Boiotia dominated by their hated rival Thebes, to a genuine belief that their gallantry might give valuable time for their own women and children to evacuate Thespiai.

Yet the Thespians do seem to have been endowed with stubborn courage: later they are said to have chosen to stand firm and face destruction on at least two other occasions – at Delion in 424 BC (Thucydides 4.96.3) and again at the Nemea in 394 BC (Xenophon *Hellenika* 4.2.20). Whatever, of the 1,400 Greeks who stayed behind with Leonidas, the Thespian dead represent at least 50 per cent of those annihilated, a remarkable percentage when we remember that they composed only about ten per cent of the original Greek force of 7,000 hoplites (Hanson 1999).

Xerxes certainly did not forget Leonidas. Herodotos says (7.238.1) the Great King had the body of the Spartan king identified, and ordered the head to be cut off and stuck on a pole for all to see. The other Greek dead, including helot corpses, were collected and left lying in heaps until sightseeing parties from the fleet had a chance to view them. However, Xerxes' attempt to conceal his own losses – he had hastily buried all but 1,000 of the 20,000 killed (Herodotos 8.24.1) – fooled nobody. Perhaps the Persian losses were not as high as 20,000, as Lazenby (1993: 148) points out, but they were certainly higher than 1,000. A humiliation for one king, Thermopylae had been another's finest hour.

Having inspired writers of all times, good and bad alike, since Simonides and Herodotos, Thermopylae is a golden story that has been often told. In more recent times there has been the full-length graphic novel adaptation of the powerful Hollywood film *The Three Hundred Spartans* (1962), published as *Lion of Sparta* (1963), an uninspired hackwork, while the five-part *Three Hundred* (1998) is rather a mixed bag. Fortunately for us moderns, there is Steven Pressfield's *Gates of Fire* (1998), a stupendous epic novel crammed full of some of the best historical drama you are likely to read. The scenes of carnage and horror that accompany the clash of battle are matter-of-factly described, and are made all the more horrifying for it. War, as Pressfield's helot narrator tells it, for certain is not glamorous nor is it heroic. But in the blood-and-urine stench of infantry combat, men are capable of incredible acts of valour.

AFTER THERMOPYLAE

The destruction of the handful of men in the little rocky pass of Thermopylae opened the way for an attack on Attica. Most of central Greece now more or less willingly went over to the Persians, but the people of Thespiai and Plataia, both in Boiotia, took refuge in the Peloponnese, and now if not before, those of Attica, too, were evacuated. To meet this threat on the landward side, a large Greek army met at the Isthmus of Corinth under the command of Leonidas' brother Kleombrotos and began the construction of a fortification wall.

The Greek fleet, which had held its own only to retreat from Artemision on hearing the fate of Leonidas, took station off Salamis, and it was here that the first decisive encounter of the war took place. The Persian fleet ventured into the narrow waters between the island and the mainland, perhaps as a result of a secret but 'false' message from the Athenian admiral, Themistokles, and was severely mauled. It still possibly had more ships than the Greeks, but it was no longer battle worthy and its morale had gone. It now sailed back across the Aegean and withdrew to Anatolia, followed by Xerxes himself. There could be no doubt about it but that the place of the Great King was back in his winter palace at Sousa, his hands upon the reigns of empire.

Salamis certainly did not end the war, though in their euphoria the Greeks may have thought it did, making dedications for victory, and trying to decide who was to receive prizes for their part in it. But the Persian army, now swelled by the medizing Greeks of Thessaly and Boiotia, still remained undefeated. So Xerxes probably left the bulk of his land forces behind, threatening Attica and the Peloponnese beyond, under his very able cousin Mardonios. He had been the leading hawk at court, a prime advocate of the epic invasion.

Yet Mardonios was more than a hardline general; he was a strategist and a diplomat. Wintering in Thessaly, Mardonios, in his capacity as satrap-designate of Greece, tried by diplomatic means to woo Athens to his side, and when this failed, marched south again in the early summer, compelling the re-evacuation of Attica for Salamis. A second embassy, this time to Salamis, failed to win the Athenians over, but Spartan procrastination almost succeeded where Persian diplomacy had failed, and at one point Athens actually threatened to make peace with the Persians. In the end the Spartans realized their defences across the Isthmus, a rugged neck of land that narrows to a width of about 8km, would not save them if the Athenian navy passed under Persian control. It might be another Thermopylae. So they mobilized their army, not under the command of Kleombrotos this time, for he had recently passed away, but under Pausanias, his son, who held the regency for his cousin Pleistarchos, the son of Leonidas.

The Delphic Column at the Hippodrome, Istanbul. Taking the form of a bronze column representing three intertwined serpents, the missing heads once supported a golden tripod. On their coils can still be seen the names of 31 Greek peoples that 'waged the war'. It was dedicated from the spoils of Plataia to Apollo at Delphi. (Author's collection)

1. Leotychides of Sparta leaves the fleet-headquarters at Delos and sails to Samos; from there the Greek fleet crosses over to Cape Mykale where the Persians have beached their ships under the protection of their army.
2. Having decided to break up the Persian floating bridges, the Greek fleet sails to the Hellespont.
3. On reaching Abydos the Greeks find that the bridges have already disintegrated; Leotychides and the Peloponnesians sail back to Greece, but the Athenians under Xanthippos remain to besiege Sestos.

Mardonios spends winter 480/479 BC in Thessaly

Xerxes sacks Athens

Plataia, August 479 BC

Land and sea engagement at Cape Mykale

Salamis, September 480 BC

Persian fleet 480 BC
Greek fleet 479 BC

On the failure of his attempts to overcome Greek opposition by manipulating the diverse interests of political factions and rival states, Mardonios fell back to Boiotia as it offered him a friendly base, abundant supplies and excellent cavalry country. It was here, just outside Plataia, that the final encounter took place, probably in the month now known as August, when the largest army of hoplites ever assembled – some 38,700 according to Herodotos (9.29.1) – annihilated the bulk of Mardonios' Asiatic troops. The 'Dorian spear' had soundly beaten the Persian 'bridle and bow', and the death of Mardonios, conspicuous on his white charger and 'surrounded by his thousand Persian troops, the flower of the army' (Herodotos 9.63.1), had decided the issue once and for all.

In the end, the Greeks won, not by brilliant strategy or tactics, or superior training and equipment, but because, in the two battles that mattered, the Persians allowed themselves to be drawn into a kind of fighting that did not suit them. At Salamis, the ribbon of water in which the engagement was fought nullified their numerical superiority – if they still had it – and hampered the speed and manoeuvrability of their ships. Xerxes was compromised and his navy broken. At Plataia, when he had the enemy on the run, Mardonios blundered into a confrontation that suited hoplites far better than his own more mobile, missile-armed troops. The struggle on the field of Plataia thus ended up as a soldier's battle rather than one directed by generals, and Mardonios lost both his army and his life.

The real reason for the Persian defeat, therefore, was that given by Corinthian envoys at a congress held in Sparta on the eve of a new and even more destructive conflict, the Peloponnesian War: 'the Barbarian failed mostly by his own fault' (Thucydides 1.69.5). Not quite Herodotos' view (7.139.5), as he preferred to stress the Athenian contribution and sacrifice, but still a very valid point nonetheless. No able general would have fruitlessly battered head on for two whole days at Thermopylae. Of course, once Xerxes got a hold on Ephialtes he reacted in the correct manner. His soldiers, on the other hand, fought loyally although they had no political rights, no democratic freedom to inspire them. In this respect the Persians refute so many of the popular stereotypes about soldiers and the human condition.

As for Ephialtes, he fled to Thessaly in fear for his life. A price had been put on his head and although he was eventually killed in a private quarrel by another man from Trachis, the Spartans nevertheless gave the bounty money to his killer (Herodotos 7.213.2).

The defeat of Xerxes was a critical event in forging a strong sense of Greek cultural and ethnic identity that was to contribute to an abiding sense that Greeks and 'barbarians' were separated by an almost unbridgeable gulf. It was quickly conceptualized, especially in Athens, as an ideological struggle between despotism and freedom, luxury and poverty. It soon took on mythical proportions and its importance is marked by the fact that it is associated with the development of the building on a large scale of the first permanent victory monuments, as well as a flood of poetry and plays celebrating and glorifying the Greek victory. Its lasting significance is demonstrated by the fact that almost a half-century later Athenian speakers could point to their service in the war against the Persians as a justification for their imperial position over other Greek states. To most people, Greece's great saviour was in the present its great enslaver.

Freedom is, above all, democratic and, as Sophokles put it, 'free men have free tongues' (fr. 927a Lloyd-Jones). At home, democratic Athens stood for freedom and equality. The Athenians even had their triremes named *Dēmokratia* (Democracy), *Eleutheria* (Freedom), and *Parrhēsia* (Free Speech). Abroad, imperial Athens did not hesitate to use any means necessary in order to enforce its authority throughout the 'island empire' that it ruled. This was the most powerful empire yet known in Greek history, and it was their navy, Themistokles' legacy, that was the weapon by which the Athenians achieved and maintained their power and prosperity. After making a stand against Xerxes in the name of freedom, Athens had discovered that in order to maintain its freedom at home, it would have to make difficult compromises abroad.

THE BATTLEFIELD TODAY

The brave 'lion king' Leonidas fittingly crowns the Thermopylae monument. Bearded, but with a moustache-free upper lip, a typically Spartan attribute, he looks out towards the battlefield from deep-socketed eyes with defiant aggression. It was there that he perished in the ranks, fighting alongside his men like a warrior chieftain. (Author's collection)

The terrain of Greece, by and large, has changed very little since antiquity, but it requires an effort of the imagination today to see the pass at Thermopylae as it was when Leonidas reached it and met his eternally remembered death. Now the relentless traffic of the National Highway thunders through the pass and there are salt flats where once was sea. Over the centuries the Malian Gulf has silted up and the modern coastline now lies several kilometres away from the scene of the action. In 480 BC, however, the point that was chosen for the defensive line was close to the sea's edge and barely 15m across in its central section, the Middle Gate. The modern road coincides with the ancient road for most of the way, except at the critical narrows where it runs north of the old course. Here the visitor has to imagine the road nearer the mountains with the sea extending to within a few metres of their foot.

The mound of the last stand, rising some 15m above the battlefield and known locally as the hillock of Kolonos, was identified for certain by Marinatos in 1939, just where Herodotos said it was, close to the road and just inside the Phokian wall. In the sandy soil Marinatos found large numbers of arrowheads, mostly of the three-edged socketed type used by the Persians, one spearhead, probably Persian, and one butt-spike, probably Greek.

Sadly the stone lion seen by Herodotos has long gone, but there are three modern monuments at the Thermopylae battlefield. Here in 1955 King Paul of the Hellenes inaugurated the memorial to the Three Hundred, a white marble monument surmounted by a striking bronze figure of a 'heroically nude' Leonidas. The base bears scenes from the battle and records the king's laconic response to Xerxes' demand that the Greeks lay down their arms. It was erected, at American expense, by the Hellenic government not far from the low hillock where the Greeks made their last stand. The second monument, actually on the site of the last stand and apparently a copy of the original, is an unadorned pink marble slab engraved with the famous words of Simonides, those which make up the shortest, and best remembered, of all his epitaphs. The third, and most recent (1996), is a Picasso-like bronze celebrating the extraordinary valour of the oft-forgotten Thespians.

BIBLIOGRAPHY

Anderson, J.K. *Xenophon* (London, Duckworth, 1974).

Anderson, M. 'The imagery of The Persians', *Greece & Rome* 19: 166–74 (1972).

Balcer, J.M. 'The Persian wars against Greece: a reassessment'. *Historia* 38: 127–43 (1989).

Bradford, E. *Thermopylae: The Battle for the West* (New York, De Capo Press, 1980).

Briant, P. (trans. Daniels, P.T.) *From Kyros to Alexander: A History of the Persian Empire*. (Warsaw, IN, Eisenbrauns, 2002).

Brosius, M. *The Persian Empire from Cyrus II to Artaxerxes I* (London, London Association of Classical Teachers [LACTOR 16], 2000).

Burn, A.R. *Persia and the Greeks: The Defence of the West,* c. *546–478 BC* (London:, Duckworth, 1962, 2nd edition 1984).

Cameron, G.G. *Persepolis Treasury Tablets* (Chicago, University of Chicago Press, 1948).

Cartledge, P.A. *The Spartans: An Epic History* (London, Channel 4 Books, 2002).

Cassin-Scott, J. *The Greek and Persian Wars, 500–323 BC*, Men-at-Arms 69 (Oxford, Osprey Publishing Ltd, 1977).

Cook, J.M. *The Persian Empire* (London, Dent, 1983).

Curtis, J. *Ancient Persia* (Cambridge, MA, Harvard University Press, 1990).

Dandamaev, M. *A Political History of the Achaemenid Empire* (New York, E.J. Brill, 1989).

De Souza, P. *The Greek and Persian Wars, 499–386 BC*, Essential Histories 36 (Oxford, Osprey Publishing Ltd, 2003).

Evans, J.A.S. 'The final problem at Thermopylai'. *Greek, Roman & Byzantine Studies* 5: 231–37, (1964).

Evans, J.A.S. 'Notes on Thermopylae and Artemision'. *Historia* 18: 389–406 (1969).

Everson, T. *Warfare in Ancient Greece: Arms and Armour from the Heroes of Homer to Alexander the Great* (Stroud, Sutton, 2004).

Fields, N. *Ancient Greek Warship, 500–322 BC*, New Vanguard 132 (Oxford, Osprey Publishing Ltd. 2007).

Frye, R.N. *The History of Persia* (London, Weidenfeld & Nicholson, 1962).

Grant, J.R. 'Leonidas' last stand'. *Phoenix* 15: 14–27 (1961).

Green, P. *The Greco-Persian Wars* (London, University of California Press, 1996).

Grundy, G.B. *The Great Persian War and its Preliminaries: A Study of the Evidence, Literary and Topographical* (London, John Murray, 1901).

Hallock, R.T. *Persepolis Fortification Tablets* (Chicago, University of Chicago Press, 1969).

Hanson, V.D. *The Western Way of War: Infantry Battle in Classical Greece* (London, Hodder & Stoughton, 1989).

Hanson, V.D. (ed.) *Hoplites: The Classical Greek Battle Experience* (London, Routledge, 1991/1993).

Hanson, V.D. 'Hoplite obliteration: the case of the town of Thespiai', in J. Carman and A.F. Harding (eds.), *Ancient Warfare: Archaeological Perspectives* pp. 203–17 (Stroud, Sutton, 1999).

Head, D. *The Achaemenid Persian Army* (Stockport, Montvert, 1992).

Hignett, C. *Xerxes' Invasion of Greece* (Oxford, Oxford University Press, 1963).

Hope Simpson, R. 'Leonidas' decision'. *Phoenix* 26: 1–11 (1972).

How, W.W. 'Arms, tactics and the strategy of the Persian War'. *Journal of Hellenic Studies* 43: 117–32 (1923).

Jameson, M.H. 'A Decree of Themistokles from Troizen'. *Hesperia* 29: 198–223 (1960).

Jameson, M.H. 'Waiting for the barbarian: new light on the Persian Wars'. *Greece & Rome* 8: 5–18 (1961).

Keegan, J. *The Mask of Command* (London, Cape, 1987).

Lazenby, J.F. 'The strategy of the Greeks in the opening campaign of the Persian War'. *Hermes* 92: 264–84 (1964).

Lazenby, J.F. *The Spartan Army* (Warminster, Aris & Phillips, 1985).

Lazenby, J.F. *The Defence of Greece, 490–479 BC* (Warminster, Aris & Phillips, 1993).

Lewis, D.M. *Sparta and Persia* (Leiden, E.J. Brill, 1977).

Lewis, D.M. 'The Persepolis Fortification Texts', in H. Sancisi-Weerdenburg and A. Kurht (eds.), *Achaemenid History IV: Centre and Periphery*, pp.1–6 (Leiden, Nederlands Instituut vor het Nabije Oosten, 1990).

Krentz, P. 'Fighting by the rules: the invention of the hoplite *agon*'. *Hesperia* 71: 23–39 (2002).

Lloyd, A. *Marathon: the Crucial Battle that Created Western Democracy* (London, Souvenir Press, 1973 and 2004).

Marinatos, S. *Thermopylae: An Illustrated Pamphlet* (Athens, 1951).

Maurice, F. 'The size of the army of Xerxes in the invasion of Greece, 480 BC'. *Journal of Hellenic Studies* 50: 210–35 (1930).

Olmstead, A.T. *History of the Persian Empire* (Chicago, University of Chicago Press, 1948, 3rd edition 1960).

Pritchett, W.K. 'New light on Thermopylae'. *American Journal of Archaeology* 62: 203–13 (1958).

Pritchett, W.K. *Studies in Ancient Greek Topography*, vols. 1–5 (Berkeley and Los Angeles, University of California Press, 1965–85).

Root, M.C. *The King and Kingship in Achaemenid Art: Essays on the Creation of an Iconography of Empire* (Leiden, E.J. Brill, 1979 – Acta Iranica 3/9).

Sacks, K.S. 'Herodotus and the dating of the battle of Thermopylae'. *Classical Quarterly* 26: 232–48 (1976).

Sage, M.M. *Warfare in Ancient Greece: A Sourcebook* (London, Routledge, 1996).

Sekunda N.V. 'The Persians', in J. Hackett (ed.) *Warfare in the Ancient World*, pp.82–103 (London, Guild Publishing, 1989).

Sekunda, N.V. *The Persian Army, 560–330 BC*, Elite 42 (Oxford, Osprey Publishing Ltd, 1992).

Sekunda, N.V. *Greek Hoplite, 480–323 BC*, Warrior 27 (Oxford: Osprey Publishing Ltd, 2000).

Strauss B. *Salamis: the Greatest Naval Battle of the Ancient World, 480 BC* (London, Hutchinson, 2004).

Usher, S. *Herodotos, the Persian Wars: A Companion* (Bristol, Bristol Classical Press, 1988).

Van Wees, H. *Greek Warfare: Myths and Realities* (London, Duckworth, 2004).

Vogelsang, W.J. *The Rise and Organization of the Achaemenid Empire* (New York, E.J. Brill, 1992).

Wallace, P.W. 'The Anopaia Path at Thermopylai'. *American Journal of Archaeology* 84: 15–23 (1980).

Wardman, A.E. 'Tactics and the tradition of the Persian Wars'. *Historia* 8: 49–60 (1959).

Young, T.C., Jnr. '480/479 BC – a Persian perspective'. *Iranica Antiqua* 15: 213–39 (1980).

INDEX

References to illustrations are shown in **bold**.